WHERE ARE THEY NOW?

WAITING FOR . . . A VISITOR

One beautiful sunny day, Samuel Beckett was told by a friend that such weather made one glad to be alive. "Oh, I wouldn't go that far," answered Beckett. In fact, since 1989, the playwright hasn't gone far at all. You can find him at Montparnasse Cemetery in Paris.

SO GO, ALREADY

Though most of these resting places are considered permanent, spiritualist Edgar Cayce claimed that he would only be passing time in Riverside Cemetery in Hopkinsville, Kentucky. Before his death in 1945, the "sleeping psychic" predicted that he would wake up in 1998—just in time to save the planet.

HER FINAL CURTAIN CALL

The actress Sarah Bernhardt rehearsed for death for years by sleeping in a coffin. Since 1923, she's been performing the role for real at Père Lachaise Cemetery in Paris.

■

"*I savored each and every entry and enjoyed it from beginning to end.*" —TERRENCE MCNALLY,
author of ... Johnny

DAVID CROSS ... ul Bear Bookstore in El ... ROBERT BENT is a free-lance journalist specializing in self-help topics. Driven by their inherent fascination for the slightly bizarre, the authors traveled to the world-renowned Père Lachaise cemetery, where they made two important discoveries: the location of the final resting place of Gertrude Stein, and the need for a book like *Dead Ends*. They are presently at work on a second volume.

DAVID CROSS
AND
ROBERT BENT

DEAD
ENDS

AN IRREVERENT FIELD GUIDE
TO THE GRAVES OF THE FAMOUS

■

A PLUME BOOK

PLUME
Published by the Penguin Group
Penguin Books USA Inc., 375 Hudson Street,
New York, New York 10014, U.S.A.
Penguin Books Ltd, 27 Wrights Lane,
London W8 5TZ, England
Penguin Books Australia Ltd, Ringwood,
Victoria, Australia
Penguin Books Canada Ltd, 10 Alcorn Avenue,
Toronto, Ontario, Canada M4V 3B2
Penguin Books (N.Z.) Ltd, 182–190 Wairau Road,
Auckland 10, New Zealand

Penguin Books Ltd, Registered Offices:
Harmondsworth, Middlesex, England

First published by Plume, an imprint of New American Library,
a division of Penguin Books USA Inc.

First Printing, October, 1991
10 9 8 7 6 5 4 3 2 1

Ⓟ Registered Trademark—Marca Registrada

Library of Congress Cataloging-in-Publication Data
Cross, David, 1948–
    Dead ends : an irreverent field guide to the graves of the famous
/ David Cross and Robert Bent.
        p. cm.
    ISBN 0-452-26679-3
    1. Celebrities—Biography—Dictionaries.   2. Celebrities—Burial—
Dictionaries.   I. Bent, Robert Freeman.   II. Title.
CT105.C8 1991
920.02—dc20
                                                                    91-9234
                                                                      CIP

Printed in the United States of America
Set in Century Expanded

Designed by Steven N. Stathakis

BOOKS ARE AVAILABLE AT QUANTITY DISCOUNTS WHEN
USED TO PROMOTE PRODUCTS OR SERVICES. FOR INFOR-
MATION PLEASE WRITE TO PREMIUM MARKETING DIVI-
SION, PENGUIN BOOKS USA INC., 375 HUDSON STREET, NEW
YORK, NEW YORK 10014.

For Alice and Gertrude

EITHER THIS MAN IS DEAD
OR MY WATCH HAS STOPPED.

—GROUCHO MARX

ACKNOWLEDGMENTS

The authors would like to thank the following people for their help and support: John Sabol, Jennifer Cecil, Alice Carey, Leonard Deaso, Melody Cagney, Gene Descoteau, Philippe Berard, and Greg Cheplin.

INTRODUCTION

The people in this book are cultural icons; they are our heroes, fantasy lovers, nightmares, and role models who have become our symbols of success, failure, good, or evil. As we look over this pantheon of more than five hundred famous and infamous names, we are surprised to see that those who shaped our somewhat puritanical civilization were by and large nonconformists in the extreme. They came in all colors, shapes, and sizes, and faced the world with little on their side but talent and determination. Many of them drank to excess, consumed illicit drugs, abandoned spouses and family, and indulged in a variety of sexual practices that still seem shocking today, decades after the sexual revolution. In short, they were individuals first, people who served themselves and their public with little or no thought given to what might be viewed as acceptable behavior once they were off the stage or set, or out of the closet.

It is often said that biography is one part truth, two parts fiction; what we believe to be true is often a reflection of our own perceptions as well as actual fact. Although we have done our best to fill these pages with an accurate history of the lives of the famous, we have not ignored the biographer's traditional sources: rumor, innuendo, and gossip. The consequences of fame include the loss of privacy and anonymity, combined with often unwelcome notoriety created by political rivals, ex-lovers, spouses, and disgruntled offspring. The sum total of an individual's life cannot be gleaned from a biographical sketch, just as an epitaph and a name with dates cannot hope to encompass more than a glimpse of the person it hopes to explain.

The loss people feel at the passing of a loved-one is magnified when that person is a public figure of mythic proportions. The grief caused by the death of a cultural hero close to our hearts often sweeps through the public consciousness, manifesting itself in a united display of mourning. Several thousand mourners rioted in the streets of New York when the body of Rudolph Valentino was on display; millions grieved for Martin Luther King, Jr., and the Kennedy brothers; and ordinary citizens the world over were shocked by the murder of John Lennon.

This book began with a pilgrimage to the grave of Gertrude Stein and Alice B. Toklas, the great American expatriates who taught us to love Paris and to love art; women who were, in Stein's own words, "busy creating the twentieth century." Carrying some flowers and a bottle of wine, we entered the gates of Père Lachaise Cemetery as if we were preparing to visit old friends. Facing the headstone for the first time, we sensed a connection we had not felt before, and as we toasted the women who had touched our hearts and minds, an aura of intimacy prevailed. At that moment, we understood the real purpose of visiting the final resting places of the dead; it may be the closest we can ever come to those people we have never met and who have changed our lives in some unforgettable way.

With *Dead Ends* as your guide, the final resting places of the famous are no longer a secret. We hope that the information contained in the pages that follow will encourage our readers to discover the joys of a pilgrimage. Whether it be Elvis Presley's Graceland, Paris's Père Lachaise, Arlington National Cemetery, or whether you prefer to stay at home and use this book as an armchair guide, we trust you will be rewarded by the wealth of information contained herein. A geographical index is included in order to make your travels more enlightening, both in the United States and abroad. It would have been impossible to include everybody's favorite personality, and some names are missing from this book for the simple reason that the grave could not be located. To correct such omissions, we welcome verifiable information from our readers.

DAVID CROSS   ROBERT BENT

KEY TO THE SYMBOLS

ANIMALS		POLITICS	
ART		RADIO	
BUSINESS		RELIGION	
CRIME		SCIENCE	
FILM		SPORTS	
HISTORY		TELEVISION	
LITERATURE		THEATER	
MUSIC			

DEAD
ENDS

BUD ABBOTT
1896—1974

"Straight" man to his partner Lou Costello, Abbott was the skinny half of the comedy duo that kept America laughing for decades with their classic routine, "Who's on first?" Their huge success in films faltered in the transition to television and soon thereafter their partnership ended with an acrimonious "divorce."

CREMATED: Ashes scattered in the Pacific Ocean

■

ANSEL ADAMS
1902—1984

Along with Strand and Stieglitz, he is credited with elevating photography to an art form. A dedicated conservationist, he felt that his pictures of the natural world might inspire others to preserve the wilderness and once said, "A photograph is not an accident; it is a concept." Apart from spending most of his adult life living and working in the outdoors, he was an accomplished self-taught pianist and teacher.

CREMATED: Ashes scattered off Half Dome, Yosemite Valley, California

■

LOUISA MAY ALCOTT
1832—1888

Born into poverty, she took up writing to make enough money to support her family. Surrounded by friends like Ralph Waldo Emerson and Henry David Thoreau, she started her career first as a journalist. When the Civil War began, she enlisted as a nurse and after the war published her journals under the title *Hospital Sketches*, a book that brought her fame and a steady income. Turning to novels, she penned the American classic *Little Women*, which became an instant success.

BURIED: Sleepy Hollow Cemetery, Concord, Massachusetts

HORATIO ALGER
1832—1899

Author of over a hundred juvenile novels, this Unitarian minister and almost-graduate of Harvard Divinity School (the day before graduation he left for Paris) rose from "rags to riches," which was the subject of all his books. Living in New York City in a home for foundling boys for over thirty years, he started his rise to success with *Ragged Dick* and went on to sell twenty million copies of his books in America. Unhappy in love, he left New York City and moved to Massachusetts, where he died alone.

BURIED: Glenwood Cemetery, South Natick, Massachusetts

GRACIE ALLEN
1906—1964

The wife and sidekick of George Burns, her wacky on-screen personality remains the epitome of the bird-brained comic. She was also the perfect foil for her husband's wry humor. First successful in vaudeville and then radio, this comedy team of Burns and Allen continues to make audiences laugh thanks to television reruns.

BURIED: Forest Lawn, Glendale, California

■

SUSAN B. ANTHONY
1820—1906

The most vocal and successful proponent of women's rights America has ever known began her political journey fighting for the abolition of slavery. She was arrested for voting in 1872 after forming the National Women's Suffrage Association. Miss Anthony never married, and she dedicated her life to winning women the right to vote. In her last speech she said, "Failure is impossible." It was a full fourteen years after her death that women were finally granted the right to vote.

BURIED: Mt. Hope Cemetery, Rochester, New York

■

MARIE ANTOINETTE
1755—1793

The original "party girl," who was also Queen of France, danced during the French Revolution, never really said, "Let them eat cake," but she was guillotined for her extravagant life-style just after the blade dropped on her husband, Louis XVI.

BURIED: Chapelle Explatoire, Paris, France

■

JOHNNY APPLESEED
1774—1845

Born John Chapman in Massachusetts, Appleseed considered himself a religious mystic who had been told by God to plant apple seeds along the route of westward migration. Starting in Ohio, he planted trees all the way to Indiana, often wearing a tin plate as a hat.

BURIED: City Utilities Park, Fort Wayne, Indiana

■

FATTY ARBUCKLE
1887—1933

Fatty (and he was) Arbuckle's career as a comic star of the silent screen was ruined after he was accused and indicted for sexually assaulting a young starlet with a cola bottle. Even though he was acquitted of all charges, he was blackballed as an actor by the still-fledgling industry. Nevertheless, he continued his film career, directing under the name William Goodrich.

BURIED: Woodlawn Cemetery, Bronx, New York

■

HANNAH ARENDT
1906—1975

A German-born writer and political activist, Arendt became the mistress of the existential philosopher Heidegger when she was still a student, surrounding herself with some of the great thinkers of the twentieth century. The essential work of her life was devoted to the Holocaust after she herself survived a Nazi internment camp. Adored by her peers, she still managed to cause a furor among intellectuals by publishing "Eichmann in Jerusalem" in *The New Yorker*, a personal reflection on the war criminal's trial, in which she coined her most famous phrase, "The banality of evil."

BURIED: Bard College, Annandale-on-Hudson, New
    York

■

LOUIS ARMSTRONG
1900—1971

Born on the fourth of July at the turn of the century, he was one of the first black superstars. His career spanned generations of music lovers, and his music crossed the color line. Part of the reason for his success in the white world may have been his refusal to speak out against the injustice of racism in America; he limited his comments to music. Nicknamed "Satchmo," his husky, original, and unforgettable voice was no doubt intensified by his legendary use of marijuana daily.

BURIED: Flushing Cemetery, New York, New York

MARY ASTOR
1906—1987

The Hollywood star, famous for "taking the fall" in *The Maltese Falcon*, won an Oscar for another film released the same year, *The Great Lie*, with Bette Davis. She was very active sexually, and when portions of her diary were published, the public was horrified. Looking for a way to retire from films gracefully, she found her answer in *Hush, Hush, Sweet Charlotte* (again with Bette); after reading the script

22

and noting that her character would be killed, she took the part, was murdered on celluloid, and left Hollywood.

BURIED: Holy Cross Cemetery, Culver City, California

■

W. H. AUDEN
1907—1973

Born, raised and educated in England, Auden became an American citizen in 1946. His absence from England during World War II tarnished his British reputation while his influence on a younger generation grew in the States. An avowed homosexual, he married Thomas Mann's daughter Erika in order to give her the British citizenship necessary for her to escape Nazi Germany. When his mother died in 1941, his work turned away from the political toward the spiritual. With his lover, Chester Kallman, he lived on the Lower East Side of New York City, the hotbed of radicalism in the 1960s, until his sudden death at their summer home in Austria.

BURIED: The cemetery at Kirchstatten, Austria

■

JOHN JAMES AUDUBON
1785—1851

He was the master illustrator of *The Birds of North America*, a three-volume work that took seven years to publish. Most of his life was spent in relative obscurity, creating the most complete and preeminent catalog of natural-history illustrations the world has ever known. Even though he died more than a century ago, his work has remained unequaled.

BURIED: Trinity Cemetery, New York, New York

■

JANE AUSTEN
1775—1817

Like Emily Dickinson in America, this English novelist spent her entire life as a spinster, living at home with her rather large family (seven children). Author of *Pride and Prejudice* and *Sense and Sensibility* among other notable works, this secretive woman reached millions of readers and continues to do so nearly two centuries after her books were first published.

BURIED: Winchester Cathedral, Winchester, England

■

JIM BACKUS
1913—1989

Without ever seeing his face, America fell in love with him as the cartoon voice of Mr. Magoo. Backus was a multitalented man, appearing in the drama *Rebel Without a Cause* with James Dean and doing comedy on television programs like "I Married Joan" and "Gilligan's Island."

BURIED: Westwood Village Memorial Park, Los Angeles, California

PEARL BAILEY
1918—1990

The "Ambassador of Love," this singer and actress reached the pinnacle of her career by starring in an all-black production of *Hello, Dolly!* on Broadway for two years. Starting out in vaudeville, she was a devoted entertainer from the old school who practiced what she preached by giving her best at every performance. Privately connected with no particular political party, she nevertheless supported several Republican presidents by appearing often at the White House. In spite of the fact that she was part African-American, part Native American, married to a white man, and known for filling her songs with sexual innuendo, she was a much-loved American entertainer; her talent apparently enabled her to transcend the racism and sexual puritanism of her country. In addition to her nightclub performances, "Pearlie Mae" also made several films, including *Porgy and Bess*.

BURIED: Rolling Green Memorial Park, West Chester, Pennsylvania

■

JAMES BALDWIN
1924—1987

Raised in Harlem, the writer James Baldwin became a preacher at the age of fifteen, abandoned the church, and became the voice of his generation. In his essay "The Fire Next Time" he warned the white power structure that black people would take by force what they could not get through social change. Then, in one of his many novels, *Giovanni's Room*, he broke through another barrier, that of his homosexuality, and in so doing instilled pride in a minority that had suffered much contempt. When he left America to settle in France, his grace, charm, and political commitment intact, he left a void in American letters that has yet to be filled. His striking looks and personal magnetism were revealed through wide, expressive eyes that drew attention to his warmth and brilliance.

BURIED: Ferncliff Cemetery, Hartsdale, New York

■

LUCILLE BALL
1911—1989

This is the woman who many consider to have been the funniest comedienne in the history of television. Starring opposite her Cuban-born husband, Desi Arnaz, on the long-running "I Love Lucy," she proved each week that she would do virtually anything for a laugh. With her carrot-colored hair and her endless schemes, she continues to keep America in stitches on reruns of the show. Beginning her film career in black and white, it was rumored that Technicolor was invented in order to capture her colorful appearance. Whether teamed in movies with her comic equal, Bob Hope, or treading the boards on Broadway in *Mame*, her reputation as a comic actress seems assured to last forever.

BURIED: Forest Lawn, Glendale, California

GEORGE BALANCHINE
1904—1983

The Russian-born choreographer, who became the guiding light of the New York City Ballet and elevated the company into one of the most successful and sought-after dance groups in the world, was a ruthless and tireless taskmaster at the barre. Often accused of rejecting prospective ballerinas because they were not tall or slim enough to fit into his vision of a uniform corps, he had a penchant for courting—and sometimes marrying—his leading ballerinas. His many fans and devotees pay homage to his memory by leaving bottles of Russian vodka on his grave, while his critics continue to insist that much of his work belonged not in the hallowed halls of ballet, but rather on a Broadway stage.

BURIED: Oakland Cemetery, Sag Harbor, New York

■

HONORÉ DE BALZAC
1799—1850

Starting as a writer of Gothic pornography, working sixteen hours a day at his desk, this French man of letters wanted both fame and social prestige, receiving the former but never the latter. Hounded by his creditors for most of his life (he squandered a fortune), he spent his last fifteen years courting a Polish countess, who finally married him just before his death. His masterwork is *The Human Comedy*.

BURIED: Père Lachaise Cemetery, Paris, France

■

TALLULAH BANKHEAD
1903—1968

Greeting her guests in the nude was just one of Tallulah Bankhead's disarming habits. Daughter of Alabama congressman and, later, Speaker of the House, William Bankhead, she was an enormous star, whose stage roles in such plays as *Little Foxes* and *Dark Victory* were given to Bette Davis in the films. She did, however, achieve immortality in celluloid for using her diamond bracelet as bait while fishing for dinner in Hitchcock's *Lifeboat*. This Southern belle was famous for her devastating wit, and during a now-famous dinner party filled with Hollywood luminaries, she was asked if Montgomery Clift was gay. Her reply is the classic, "I have no idea, dahling. He never sucked my cock."

BURIED: St. Paul's Episcopal Churchyard, Chestertown, Maryland

■

P.T. BARNUM
1810—1891

While still a child, he started the first lottery in Connecticut, and as an adult he ran the New York City "American Museum" (really a freak show), which featured the famous midget General Tom Thumb and the Bearded Lady. At the age of sixty, Barnum joined his

29

rival, Bailey, to form the Barnum and Bailey Circus. When he bought Jumbo, the world's largest white elephant, from an English zoo, the incident caused an international crisis by upsetting the royal family and the British people, who adored the animal. Known for his caustic tongue, he once told a newsman as they surveyed his giant big top, which held twenty thousand people per show, "There's an asshole for every seat."

BURIED: Mountain Grove Cemetery, Bridgeport, Connecticut

■

CLYDE BARROW
1909—1934

In addition to robbing banks, gas stations, and grocery stores, Clyde murdered most of his holdup victims with the help of his sidekick and lover, Bonnie Parker. This renegade duo eluded police throughout the South, and when captured, often escaped. The famous criminal John Dillinger called them "a couple of punks" who gave bank robbers a bad name. On the day their murderous spree came to an end, the police unloaded 187 rounds of ammunition on them, killing the couple but not their reputation.

BURIED: West Dallas Cemetery, Dallas, Texas

■

ETHEL BARRYMORE
1879—1959

The female member of the Barrymore acting trio appeared with her brothers, John and Lionel, in only one film, *Rasputin and the Empress*. Her other screen roles were few, but she was considered a great star. With her roots in vaudeville, she never deserted the theater and dreamed of becoming a pianist. She will long be remembered for playing the teacher in *The Corn Is Green*.

BURIED: Mt. Vernon Cemetery, Philadelphia, Pennsylvania

■

JOHN BARRYMORE
1882—1942

He was the most emotional and unstable of the Barrymores, but he was also considered the greatest American Hamlet of the twentieth century. Appearing with Garbo in *Grand Hotel*, he became a matinee idol on the screen as well as on the stage. The last part of his career was marred by alcoholism, making it impossible for him to remember his lines, and toward the end he turned to radio, where he was able to read from the script. Like all the Barrymores, he did not want to act; he wanted to become a painter.

BURIED: Mt. Vernon Cemetery, Philadelphia, Pennsylvania

■

LIONEL BARRYMORE
1878—1954

Although he loathed acting and was confined to a wheelchair for most of his career, he made over seventy films, not including the Dr. Kildare series. In his later life he became a composer of serious music, and one of his compositions was performed by the New York Philharmonic.

BURIED: Calvary Cemetery, Los Angeles, California

■

CHARLES BAUDELAIRE
1821—1867

A poet of remorse, the French dandy and aristocrat liked women of color and wrote sensual poems about his fixations. A prophet of sorts, his poem *An Opium Eater* was a precursor to the work of Freud; it details the importance of early childhood. Dogged by creditors for most of his life, he wrote a series of humorous essays, the most famous being "How to Pay Your Debts When You Are a Genius." He is considered to be the first art critic and published the first collection of what is now called modern poetry.

BURIED: Montparnasse Cemetery, Paris, France

■

AUBREY BEARDSLEY
1872—1898

Tubercular as a child, Beardsley lived to be only twenty-five, but in that short time he managed to become one of the most notorious artists of the day. He sold his first drawing at age ten and illustrated *Morte d'Arthur* at twenty, with the latter considered a masterpiece. Next came illustrations for Oscar Wilde's *Salomé* (Wilde hated the drawings), and his fame was assured. Terribly self-conscious of his height (he was six-feet six-inches tall), he dyed his hair green and remarked, "If I am not grotesque, I am nothing." After Oscar Wilde was arrested for sodomy, Beardsley's career plummeted, and no one would publish his work. He promptly converted to Catholicism and died. His influence on Art Nouveau was immense, and his pornographic drawings were later published despite his express wish to have them destroyed.

BURIED: Cathedral Cemetery, Menton, France

■

SIMONE DE BEAUVOIR
1908—1986

When she published *The Second Sex*, de Beauvoir became an intellectual leader of the feminist movement worldwide, and she remains, even after her death, a source of inspiration. Saying "One is not born a woman, one becomes one," she vowed to create her own life and did so by adopting a bohemian life-style and creating a towering body of thought and work, including *The Ethics of Ambiguity* and *The Mandarins*. Allying herself with Jean-Paul Sartre in a relationship that lasted for over fifty years until his death, she nonetheless had several other major love affairs, including one with the Chicago writer Nelson Algren that lasted on and off for several decades. With Sartre she visited Khrushchev in Russia and Castro in Cuba, but she later severed her connection with the Party because of what she viewed as the failure of communism. Her lengthy autobiography was published in four volumes.

BURIED: Montparnasse Cemetery, Paris, France

∎

SAMUEL BECKETT
1906—1989

Awarded the Nobel Prize for Literature in 1969, this Irish-born writer, whose bleak view of life became his trademark in such plays as *Krapp's Last Tape* and *Waiting for Godot*, spent most of his adult life in his adopted Paris, married his nurse, and after her death lived in a nursing home watching tennis on TV. When a friend once drove him to the country on a fine spring day and remarked that such weather made one glad to be alive, Beckett reportedly answered, "Oh, I wouldn't go that far."

BURIED: Montparnasse Cemetery, Paris, France

∎

WALLACE BEERY
1885—1949

Known to be as tough and ugly in person as he appeared to be in films, Beery was an enormous star who made many Hollywood classics such as *Treasure Island, Dinner at Eight,* and *Grand Hotel.*

BURIED: Forest Lawn, Glendale, California

■

LUDWIG VAN BEETHOVEN
1770—1827

His music was adored by composers as varied as Brahms and Wagner. His dream of studying with Mozart was never realized; instead, he was tutored by Haydn in Vienna, his adopted city, from which he later never traveled. Obsessed by his music, he had few friends and never married. Midway through his life he became deaf, an affliction that tortured him, exacerbating his already pronounced misanthropy and making him unbearable in public. Considered by many to be the greatest composer of all time, his work got better as he grew older and deafer.

BURIED: Central Cemetery, Vienna, Austria

■

BRENDAN BEHAN
1923—1964

Lusty, gregarious, and hard-drinking, the Irish play-wright Behan penned a modern classic called *The Hostage* and left in his wake enough barroom stories to last forever. He was loud, boisterous, and often offensively drunk, but also charismatic, brilliant, and filled with charm. He once said that if it rained soup in Ireland, his fellow countrymen would come out with forks.

BURIED: Glasnevin Cemetery, Donnybrook, Ireland

ALEXANDER GRAHAM BELL
1847—1922

Born in Scotland, Bell emigrated to Canada, where he taught the deaf and invented a device that revolutionized communications—the telephone.

BURIED: Beinn Breach Estate, Braddeck, Nova Scotia, Canada

JOHN BELUSHI
1949—1982

The heavyset Samurai comedian became a star on "Saturday Night Live," graduating into films that were box office bonanzas and teaming with Dan Ackroyd (wearing fedoras and dark glasses) to form the singing duo The Blues Brothers. Given to excess in food, drink, and drugs, this unique and funny man died mysteriously of a drug overdose that implicated those who were reportedly with him at the time of his death. To this day there remain unanswered questions concerning his tragic demise.

BURIED: Abel's Hill Cemetery, Chilmark, Martha's Vineyard, Massachusetts

■

BEA BENADERET
1894—1968

Remembered best for being the voice of Betty Rubble in *The Flintstones*, she also portrayed the slightly flustered next-door neighbor of George Burns and Gracie Allen on television.

BURIED: Valhalla Memorial Park, Burbank, California

■

JACK BENNY
1894—1974

Perennially thirty-nine, Benny tortured the violin, pinched pennies, and made his audience laugh with a deadpanned delivery, an unmistakable voice, perfect timing, and an expressive face. A major star for almost half a century, he was privately a generous man who was adored by his family, friends, and the public.

BURIED: Hillside Memorial Park, Burbank, California

■

EDGAR BERGEN
1903—1978

The Swedish-born voice of Charlie McCarthy (a dummy dressed in a tuxedo and sporting a monocle), Bergen was the most famous ventriloquist of all time. His talent and comic genius made it impossible for his audience to tell who was actually in control, man or dummy, or who was the bigger star. His daughter, actress Candice Bergen, has confessed that as a child she felt a sense of sibling rivalry with the well-known doll that sat on her father's knee.

BURIED: Inglewood Park Cemetery, Los Angeles, California

■

INGRID BERGMAN
1915—1982

The Swedish-born film star, who became the darling of American audiences in such classics as *Casablanca*, *Gaslight*, and *The Bells of St. Mary*, was a box office success. She represented motherhood and purity until she left her husband and daughter to become the lover of Italian director Roberto Rossellini, with whom she had two illegitimate children. Scorned by her fans, denounced from the church pulpits of America, and formally condemned on the Senate floor, her career seemed doomed to failure. But when she returned to Hollywood in the title role of *Anastasia*, she refused to apologize for her private choices and went on to win an Oscar, gathering back her old fans and adding millions more. One of the most beautiful women ever to appear before the camera, she bravely made *Autumn Sonata* under the direction of Ingmar Bergman, without the benefit of makeup while being treated for the cancer that finally took her life.

CREMATED: Ashes scattered at sea off the coast of her private island, Danholmen, Sweden

■

SARAH BERNHARDT
1844–1923

The irrepressible French actress, whom many considered the finest practitioner of her chosen profession, gave endless "farewell performances" in America toward the end of her life. During a tour of Rio de Janeiro—playing Tosca—she broke her leg during the suicide scene when the mattress that was to break her fall was missing. Refusing treatment in South America, she sailed for New York and consulted many physicians, only to be told that nothing could be done. After years of using small doses of morphine to ease the pain, her leg was finally amputated, a fact announced to the world in a cable reading: "Doctors will cut off my leg next Monday. Am very happy. Kisses, All my best, Sarah." At age seventy-two, after sleeping in a coffin for years, she made her *final* final farewell tour of America.

BURIED: Père Lachaise Cemetery, Paris, France

LEONARD BERNSTEIN
1918–1990

Born into a family of Russian immigrants, he was a musical prodigy who became the most famous American conductor and composer of his time. Never satisfied with one career, he wrote music for films (*On*

the Waterfront), Broadway (*West Side Story*), ballet (*Fancy Free*), and opera (*Candide*). As the music director of the New York Philharmonic, his flamboyance made him a star, and his televised "Young People's Concerts" influenced two generations of young musicians. A liberal Democrat, Bernstein's fund-raising parties, especially one given for the Black Panthers, generated heated debate, and although married and the father of three children, his homosexuality was never a secret. "Lenny's" connection to two distinctly different presidents is revealing; he wrote his *Mass* for John F. Kennedy but refused a medal from George Bush to protest the NEA's refusal to fund AIDS-related art works.

BURIED: Green-Wood Cemetery, Brooklyn, New York

∎

BILLY THE KID
1859—1881

Born in New York City, this cowboy, murderer, and legend in his own time roamed the Southwest, killing his first man at the tender age of twelve. Pursued and captured by Pat Garrett, he escaped hanging but was later shot dead in a duel. His exploits were immortalized on stage by the choreographer Agnes DeMille and the composer Aaron Copland in their ballet, *Billy the Kid*.

BURIED: The Old Fort, Fort Sumner, New Mexico

∎

CLARA BLANDICK
1881—1962

Her small but secure claim to celluloid immortality is as Dorothy's Auntie Em in *The Wizard of Oz*. At the ripe old age of eighty-one, she put on her best dress, went into her Hollywood bedroom, placed a plastic bag over her head, and committed suicide by asphyxiation.

BURIED: Forest Lawn, Glendale, California

■

HUMPHREY BOGART
1899—1957

The bulldog-faced actor personified the tough guy in films like *Key Largo*, *The Treasure of the Sierra Madre*, and *The Maltese Falcon* (in which he told a terrified Mary Astor that she was "taking the fall"). Born on Park Avenue in New York City and educated at private schools, he married Lauren Bacall after her debut as his costar in *To Have and Have Not*, when "Bogie" was forty-five and "Baby" was twenty. He won his only Oscar as the tough but gentle boat captain opposite a staunch but vulnerable Katharine Hepburn in *The African Queen*, a movie made on location under the direction of John Huston. He was an outspoken iconoclast, who said about the House Un-American Activities Committee, "They'll nail anyone who ever scratched his ass during the national anthem."

BURIED: Forest Lawn, Glendale, California

■

RAY BOLGER
1904—1987

As the Scarecrow in *The Wizard of Oz*, he danced as if his body were made not of straw but of rubber. A major star of Hollywood musicals, his theme song was "Once in Love with Amy," and he entertained the world for over half a century.

BURIED: Holy Cross Cemetery, Los Angeles, California

■

NAPOLEON BONAPARTE
1769—1821

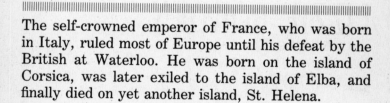

The self-crowned emperor of France, who was born in Italy, ruled most of Europe until his defeat by the British at Waterloo. He was born on the island of Corsica, was later exiled to the island of Elba, and finally died on yet another island, St. Helena.

BURIED: Les Invalides, Paris, France

■

JOHN WILKES BOOTH
1838—1865

When the Civil War came to an end, John Wilkes Booth's plan to kidnap Abraham Lincoln and force the North to surrender became quickly outdated. So the critically acclaimed actor, who served the South under Robert E. Lee, shot the president at Ford's Theatre. His own death remains a mystery; he may have killed himself, or he may have actually escaped, changed his name, and lived the rest of his days in Mexico.

BURIED: Green Mountain Cemetery, Baltimore, Maryland

■

LIZZIE BORDEN
1860—1927

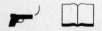

More than half a century after her death, children still know the rhyme about Lizzie giving her parents "forty whacks" with an axe. Her acquittal of the murders did little to deter the public's fascination with the still-unsolved crime.

BURIED: Oak Grove Cemetery, Fall River, Massachusetts

■

CLARA BOW
1905—1965

Born in Brooklyn, New York, she went to Hollywood as a teenager for a beauty contest and wound up making a film called *It*. Thereafter she was known as "The It Girl" and became the embodiment of film sexuality for the Jazz Age. When the talkies replaced silent films, her career came to a sudden halt; film audiences roared with laughter when they heard her Brooklyn accent.

BURIED: Forest Lawn, Glendale, California

■

CHARLES BOYER
1899—1978

"Come to the Casbah," said young Charles Boyer to the ravishing Hedy Lamarr, and from that moment on he was considered one of the silver screen's sexiest men, a position further enhanced by his role opposite Ingrid Bergman in *Gaslight*. In reality he was a devoted family man who never recovered from the suicide of his only son, and when his wife died, he took his own life.

BURIED: Holy Cross Cemetery, Culver City, California

■

BERTOLT BRECHT
1898—1956

As the longtime collaborator of Kurt Weill, his lyrics changed the course of the modern musical and redefined modern opera. Together their biggest hit was *The Threepenny Opera* starring Lotte Lenya. Although the critics in Berlin dismissed it as "Bolshevist madness," the production went on to become the most successful musical in German history, with over four thousand performances in more than a hundred theaters throughout the country. During its first run in the U.S. it closed after only thirteen performances.

BURIED: Dorotheenstadt and Friedrichswerder Cemetery, Berlin, Germany

■

FANNY BRICE
1891—1951

Discovered by Flo Ziegfeld in a burlesque house, she was the comedienne and singer who dominated the vaudeville stage before appearing in the film *The Great Ziegfeld*. Her trademark song was "My Man," and she performed with such greats as Will Rogers, W. C. Fields, and Eddie Cantor. Up until her death she was the voice of Baby Snooks on national radio. The play and film *Funny Girl*, starring Barbra Streisand, was based on her life story.

BURIED: Home of Peace Cemetery, Los Angeles, California

■

46

JOHN BROWN
1800—1859

Seen in the South as the "Devil incarnate," this passionate abolitionist dedicated his life to the freeing of slaves in America. Always in debt, and with twenty children to feed, he settled a black community in the Adirondacks and was later elected the commander of a "free state" that attacked and murdered proslavery citizens. Defeated at Harpers Ferry by Robert E. Lee, he was tried, convicted, and executed, becoming a martyr to the abolitionist movement.

BURIED: John Brown Farm, North Elba, New York

■

ELIZABETH BARRETT BROWNING
1806—1861

As a semi-invalid child of a tyrannical father, she read history and philosophy while writing poetry. Her first published collection brought her instant success. After a brief correspondence with Robert Browning, they married and moved to Italy. Their marriage was a happy one, although she was far more successful as a poet than he was.

BURIED: Cimitero degli Inglesi, Florence, Italy

■

ROBERT BROWNING
1812—1889

The English poet, who wrote plays in verse (most of them unsuccessful) and married the poet Elizabeth Barrett, was an optimistic man, whose success came late in his life. Returning to England after the death of his wife at their home in Italy, he became famous for both his dramatic monologues and the poetic masterpiece *The Ring and the Book*, a murder mystery in verse that portrays one event as perceived by four different people.

BURIED: Poet's Corner, Westminster Abbey, London, England

LENNY BRUCE
1925—1966

Dubbed "sick" by the media, this stand-up comic and social critic was discharged from the Navy for homosexuality, repeatedly arrested for using obscene language, and frequently busted for drugs. Bruce broke all the rules of public morality and achieved cult status among intellectuals opposed to the status quo. Hounded by the police and unable to perform in public, he gradually lost control of his life until he was found dead sitting on a toilet with a needle in his arm.

BURIED: Mission Hills Cemetery, Los Angeles, California

NIGEL BRUCE
1885—1958

This English actor was perfectly suited to the role of
Dr. Watson, the endearing sidekick of Sherlock
Holmes in the film series. Besides costarring in *The
Adventures of Sherlock Holmes* and *The Hound of the
Baskervilles*, he appeared in the classics *Rebecca* and
Suspicion, two Hitchcock masterpieces.

BURIED: Chapel of the Pines, Los Angeles, California

■

PEARL S. BUCK
1892—1973

Born in West Virginia but raised in China by missionary parents, she became one of the most famous nov-
elists of her time. Her book *The Good Earth* won a
Pulitzer Prize and was made into both a stage play
and an Oscar-winning film. She wrote fifty-three
books, some of them under the name John Sedges, and
later won the Nobel Prize for Literature.

BURIED: Green Hills Farm, Perkasie, Pennsylvania

■

RICHARD BURTON
1925—1984

Married to Elizabeth Taylor twice, Welsh actor Richard Burton sacrificed a promising career on the stage for the glamour and gold of Hollywood. Famous for both his commanding voice and his destructive drinking (which he eventually gave up), he left the world with several memorable screen performances in films such as *Who's Afraid of Virginia Woolf?* and *Becket.* Rather than be buried in his native Wales among his family, he chose Switzerland as his final resting place in order to avoid inheritance taxes.

BURIED: Protestant Churchyard, Celigny, Switzerland

■

SPRING BYINGTON
1893—1971

After a long and distinguished career on Broadway, she moved to Hollywood and found a perfect role in her first film, *Little Women*. Dozens of films followed, including *Mutiny on the Bounty* and *Please Don't Eat the Daisies*. During the 1950s she was a regular on "December Bride," first on radio and later on television.

BODY DONATED TO SCIENCE

■

LORD BYRON
1788—1824

Often considered one of the greatest Romantic poets, this English writer created what was to be called the Byronic hero, an independent man of determination who bears the scars of a tragic past. His masterworks include *Don Juan* and *Childe Harold*.

BURIED: Byron Family Vault, Hucknall, Nottingham, England

■

SEBASTIAN CABOT
1918—1977

This overweight British character actor became famous in films for playing the stodgy Englishman and appeared in the musical *Kismet* as well as the classic, *Ivanhoe*. In his later years he became a television star in the immensely successful sitcoms "Checkmate" and "Family Affair."

BURIED: Westwood Village Memorial Park, Los Angeles, California

■

MOTHER CABRINI
1850—1917

As a young nun from Italy, Sister Cabrini had an uncanny knack for raising money to open orphanages and schools around the world. Rewarded for her ceaseless fund-raising, she was the first American to be canonized a saint by the Roman Catholic Church.

BURIED: Cabrini High School, Port Washington, New York

■

JAMES CAGNEY
1899—1986

Cagney may have danced his way into show business and into the hearts of the American public, but it was his versatility as an actor that made him a star. Whether he was singing in *Yankee Doodle Dandy* or sneering in *Public Enemy*, he was the consummate performer, who mesmerized filmgoers for half a century.

BURIED: Gate of Heaven Cemetery, Mt. Pleasant, New York

■

MARIA CALLAS
1923—1977

The prima donna assoluta of opera, she single-handedly changed the way opera is sung in the twentieth century. Born in New York City and overweight as a young girl, her family moved to Greece, where she eventually transformed herself into a woman of exceptional beauty, slim as a model in the pages of *Vogue* magazine. A temperamental but exacting diva, her life and career were filled with controversy and tragedy, and it is said she died of a broken heart when her former lover, Aristotle Onassis, married "The Widow" Jacqueline Kennedy.

CREMATED: Ashes scattered in the Aegean Sea

■

GODFREY CAMBRIDGE
1933—1976

Probably the first black actor to play a white man (in the film *Watermelon Man*), Cambridge was a civil rights activist and comedian of West Indian heritage. His humor had an undercurrent of rage stemming from his long experience with American racism. He died from a heart attack at the age of forty-three while playing his first dramatic film role as Idi Amin in a television movie.

BURIED: Forest Lawn Hollywood Hills, Los Angeles, California

■

ALBERT CAMUS
1913—1960

Considered one of the most influential thinkers of the twentieth century, the Algerian-born writer's work is seminal to modern philosophy. His essay "The Myth of Sisyphus" illuminated his beliefs that life is absurd as well as meaningless and that individuals must find joy in the struggle of existence. Critically allied with the existential movement in his novels (*The Stranger*, *The Plague*, and *The Rebel*), he rejected that association in the end. He won the Nobel Prize for Literature in 1957 but was scorned by Sartre for not embracing Marxism and Stalinism. Camus died when his car crashed into a tree on a return trip to Paris from his new home in the South of France.

BURIED: The cemetery at Lourmarin, France

EDDIE CANTOR
1892—1964

This popeyed singer with the high voice was an enormous radio star in the 1930s. A popular guest on many television variety shows, Cantor's theme song was "If You Knew Susie," which was also the title of a less than memorable film.

BURIED: Hillside Memorial Park, Los Angeles, California

AL CAPONE
1889—1947

Who said, "Crime doesn't pay"? In Al "Scarface" Capone's case it most certainly did. When he was released from prison in 1939, he retired to his Palm Beach estate and lived off the several million dollars the government was unable to take away from him. He died of syphilis.

BURIED: Mt. Carmel Cemetery, Hillside, Illinois

TRUMAN CAPOTE
1924—1984

With his pudgy body, decidedly limp wrist, and effeminate, high-pitched voice, this genius of American letters became an unlikely television talk show celebrity while producing several modern classics as well as lots of gossip disguised as art. Keenly intelligent, alcoholic, homosexual, charming, and plagued by depression, his first novel, *Other Voices, Other Rooms*, made him a star. Turning to the stage, he wrote the book and lyrics (with music by Harold Arlen) to *House of Flowers*. His long short story *Breakfast at Tiffany's* was turned into the highly successful film starring Audrey Hepburn, and while ensconced at *The New Yorker*, Truman wrote the first "nonfiction" novel, *In Cold Blood*, which later became a disturbing film. The host of the biggest society ball of the sixties, The Black-and-

White Ball, he alienated his high-society friends by writing about their private lives in his last unfinished work, *Unanswered Prayers*. After his sad death, a one-character play, *Tru*, based on Capote's life and persona, was a hit on Broadway.

BURIED: Westwood Village Cemetery, Los Angeles, California

■

HOAGY CARMICHAEL
1899—1981

Starting out as the leader of a jazz band, he later became one of America's most beloved composers with such songs as "Stardust," "Georgia on My Mind," and "I Get Along Without You Very Well." His "Lamplight Serenade" was the first song recorded by Frank Sinatra, and he appeared in the films *To Have and Have Not* and *The Best Years of Our Lives* among others. In his later years Carmichael became the host of various radio and television shows.

BURIED: Rose Hill Cemetery, Bloomington, Indiana

■

KAREN CARPENTER
1950—1983

She was one half of the brother-and-sister singing duo
The Carpenters, whose easy-listening sound ranked
high on the charts for over a decade. Her death at the
age of thirty-three from anorexia nervosa brought this
particular medical affliction into the consciousness of
an unsuspecting public, whose young daughters were
obsessed with being thin.

BURIED: Forest Lawn-Cypress, Orange City, California

BILLY CARTER
1937—1988

Billy, the beer-drinking peanut farmer who just happened to be the brother of the president of the United
States, charmed the nation with his eccentric personality, was seduced by the power of the media, and
became a victim of his own fame by allying himself
with unscrupulous business partners who were inves-
tigated for selling arms to Libya. His final fiasco was
lending his name to an unsuccessful brew called Billy
Beer, a foul-tasting concoction that is now a collector's
item worth twelve hundred dollars a six-pack.

BURIED: Lebanon Cemetery, Plains, Georgia

LILLIAN CARTER
1898–1983

Mother of President Carter, she joined the Peace Corps at the age of sixty-eight and presided over the "Southern White House" in Georgia during her son's tenure with a combination of wit, grace, and down-home humor.

BURIED: Lebanon Cemetery, Plains, Georgia

ENRICO CARUSO
1873–1921

The "King of Tenors" was born in Naples, Italy, and lived in New York City, where he was once arrested for molesting a woman at the Central Park Zoo. A lonely man with a great voice, he defied the Mafia, had a series of painful love affairs, and finally settled into marriage (and a family), living in a luxurious suite at the Vanderbilt Hotel. While onstage during a performance, a prop struck him in the chest, and although he made it to the wings with a theatrical flourish worthy of the egotistical superstar he was, he was forced to retire to Italy, where he died soon after.

BURIED: Del Panto Cemetery, Naples, Italy

WILLIAM CASEY
1913—1987

As the head of the CIA under Ronald Reagan, Casey was the man who allegedly aided and abetted Oliver North and his cronies in Irangate, a covert operation that sold American arms to Iran and used the profits to bolster the so-called Contras in Nicaragua. He did not live long enough to face possible prosecution.

BURIED: Holyrood Cemetery, Roslyn, Long Island, New York

MARY CASSATT
1844—1926

The American expatriate and impressionist painter who showed at the Paris Salon was a protégée of Degas. Unmarried and committed to her painting, she overcame the hostile attitude toward women in the arts and forged a place of respect among her peers. Her success in France was unmatched in America, and when she returned to Philadelphia, after a twenty-eight-year absence, the press ignored her fame as a painter, reporting only that she owned the smallest pekingese dog in the world. Blind at the time of her death, she spent her last years in lonely isolation at her French château.

BURIED: The Cassatt Family Vault, near Château Beaufresne, Oise Valley, Beauvais, France

JOHN CASSAVETES
1929—1989

An American actor and director, he gave Hollywood some fine performances in other people's films before branching out on his own and directing some of the most unusual and provocative films ever made. With a circle of friends including Peter Falk, Elaine May, and his wife Gena Rowlands, this unique filmmaker explored the meaning of love and friendship in films such as *Husbands*.

BURIED: Westwood Village Memorial Park, Los Angeles, California

■

EDGAR CAYCE
1877—1945

The psychic entity who was reincarnated as Edgar Cayce lived many previous lives—or so he and his followers claimed. Either as a high priest or a king, he never seemed to incarnate as an ordinary person and in fact promised to be back in 1998, this time as the savior of the planet. He read the Bible cover to cover each year and tried to persuade Christians that reincarnation was not a device of the Devil but a teaching of Jesus. He developed an enormous following based on his alleged ability to heal illness by "reading" an individual's past life.

BURIED: Riverside Cemetery, Hopkinsville, Kentucky

■

JEFF CHANDLER
1918—1961

This nice Jewish boy from Brooklyn moved west, changed his name, shaved his hirsute body, took advantage of his prematurely gray hair, and became a Hollywood sex symbol in a series of B movies like *Broken Arrow* (in which he played the shirtless Indian Cochise) and *Yankee Pasha* (in which he broke up a fistfight between Arlene Dahl and Rhonda Fleming, the feuding redheads).

BURIED: Hillside Memorial Park, Los Angeles, California

■

RAYMOND CHANDLER
1888—1959

Born in Chicago but educated in England, Chandler began his writing career after settling in southern California. Obviously inspired in part by the work of Dashiell Hammett, he created the character Philip Marlowe, a lonely tough-guy detective who worked the streets of Los Angeles. *The Lady in the Lake*, *The Long Goodbye*, and *Farewell, My Lovely* are now considered American literary classics.

BURIED: Mount Hope Cemetery, San Diego, California

■

COCO CHANEL
1882—1971

Creator of Chanel No. 5, the first designer perfume, this French fashion designer influenced the way women dressed in both Europe and the United States for several generations. Chic, petite, and undeniably charismatic, her fitted suits were worn by corporate executives, socialites, and international celebrities such as the Duchess of Windsor and Jacqueline Kennedy Onassis. She was also known as an armchair philosopher with a habit of pronouncing fashionable bon mots, and she once said, "Life is like a toboggan ride; you get on, and you never look back."

BURIED: The cemetery at Lausanne, Switzerland

■

LON CHANEY, SR.
1883—1930

The Phantom of the Opera and *The Hunchback of Notre Dame* terrified millions of silent-film fans and made Chaney famous. A natural for the silent era, since his parents were both deaf and mute, the "Man of a Thousand Faces" did all his own makeup, devised his own costumes, and created his own special effects.

BURIED: Forest Lawn, Glendale, California

■

CHARLES CHAPLIN
1889—1977

The "Little Tramp" took America by storm in silent films and later caused a worldwide scandal by marrying a woman young enough to be his daughter, Oona O'Neill, daughter of the playwright Eugene O'Neill. Contrary to expectations the couple fared very well and remained married until Chaplin's death. Considered by many to be one of the cinema's great geniuses, he never won an Academy Award and was hounded out of the United States for his pacifist beliefs.

BURIED: The Cemetery at Corsier, Switzerland

CHECKERS

Former President Richard Nixon's cocker spaniel was made famous in a televised speech that saved the then vice-presidential nominee's political career. It is unfortunate for the nation that the emotional ploy with a sweet puppy worked so well, because the man history calls "Tricky Dick" went on to become the first president forced to resign in disgrace.

BURIED: Bide-a-Wee Pet Cemetery, Wantaugh, Long
    Island, New York

JOHN CHEEVER
1912—1982

One of the most influential of American writers, his suppressed homosexuality was reflected in his obsession with the darker underpinnings of suburbia. His own upper-middle-class appearance belied his long history of substance abuse. A fine novelist (*Falconer*), he is primarily noted for his collections of short stories, *The Wapshot Chronicles* and *The Wapshot Scandals*; both are considered American classics.

BURIED: First Parish Cemetery, Norwell, Massachusetts

ANTON CHEKHOV
1860—1904

The Russian playwright and short-story writer, who penned such classics as *The Cherry Orchard*, *The Seagull*, and *Uncle Vanya*, was terrified of women and did not marry until very old, ill, and near death. His coffin arrived for burial stamped with the words *For Oysters*, and his last words were, "It's been so long since I've had champagne."

BURIED: Novo Devich Cemetery, Moscow, USSR

MAURICE CHEVALIER
1888—1972

The French singer began in the music halls of Paris
and graduated to films, becoming an international celebrity in such classics as *Can-Can*, *Fanny*, and *Gigi*.
Tall, slim, and white-haired, he never lost his sex appeal and wooed audiences with his unmistakable voice,
his straw hat, and his light-as-a-feather soft-shoe dancing. Paired with Hermione Gingold in *Gigi*, Chevalier
was tailor-made for the songs, "I Remember It Well"
and "I'm So Glad I'm Not Young Anymore."

BURIED: Village Cemetery, Marnes La Coquette,
France

■

FRÉDÉRIC-FRANÇOIS CHOPIN
1810—1849

The Polish composer and pianist was a superstar in
the salons of Europe. His scandalous liaison with
George Sand, the power of his playing, and the over-
whelming emotional impact of his compositions gave
him the kind of fame accorded in our own time only to
movie and rock stars. Even his death at the age of

thirty-nine from tuberculosis fed the public's image of him as a romantic genius.

BURIED: Père Lachaise Cemetery, Paris, France

■

AGATHA CHRISTIE
1890—1976

The grande dame of murder mysteries, she wrote over eighty novels and the longest-running play in English theater history, *The Mousetrap*. Her most famous detective, Miss Jane Marple, has had several incarnations in films and on television, with the unforgettable Margaret Rutherford setting the tone for future portrayals and unsuspectingly creating an inaccurate image of Christie herself. British to the bone, Agatha Christie has fed the imaginations of millions and millions of readers worldwide with such books as *Witness for the Prosecution, Death on the Nile* and *Sleeping Murder*. She once disappeared without a trace, and her whereabouts during that time remains a real-life mystery for both her fans and amateur sleuths.

BURIED: Cholsey Churchyard, Cholsey, Berkshire,
England

■

WINSTON CHURCHILL
1874—1965

This rotund prime minister of England rallied his nation during World War II and was idolized by his people. Known for his unmistakable size and demeanor, his cigars, and his quick wit, he was once accosted by a woman at a party who loudly proclaimed that he was drunk. "And you, madame," he replied, "are ugly. But I shall be sober in the morning."

BURIED: Bladon Churchyard, Long Handborough, England

■

MONTGOMERY CLIFT
1920—1964

The brooding but brilliant actor, whose career took a nose dive after his near-fatal auto accident, was an unhappy homosexual whose great talent is evident in films like *The Heiress*, *A Place in the Sun*, and *From Here to Eternity*. He apparently had a vast knowledge of pharmaceuticals and a predilection for S & M parties, and it is rumored that his death resulted from mixing the two.

BURIED: Brooklyn Quaker Cemetery, Brooklyn, New York

■

PATSY CLINE
1932—1963

With the voice of an angel, this country singer quickly became a regular at the Grand Ole Opry and rose to the top of her profession by singing songs like "Crazy" and "Sweet Dreams." She died in a plane crash while touring the United States.

BURIED: Shenandoah Memorial Park, Winchester, Virginia

LEE J. COBB
1911—1976

Seemingly incapable of giving a bad performance, this towering American actor left the New York stage, where he starred in *Death of a Salesman*, and moved to Hollywood, performing in *On the Waterfront* with Brando. After appearing in many other fine films like *The Man in the Gray Flannel Suit* and *Twelve Angry Men*, he turned to television and starred in *The Virginian*.

BURIED: Mt. Sinai Memorial Park, Los Angeles, California

JEAN COCTEAU
1889—1963

Cocteau's genius was to be found in his conversation as well as his ability to dissect the society in which he lived. Writer, painter, and filmmaker, he worked in virtually every artistic medium and became a cause célèbre of the French avant-garde. His novel *Les Enfants Terribles* remains a modern classic, and his film *The Beauty and the Beast* is a masterpiece of the genre. Famous for saying that a person's final exit should not be missed (a theatrical reference to death), he missed his own by dying a few days after Edith Piaf; the whole of France was in mourning and his death was barely noticed.

BURIED: Milly La Forêt Cemetery, Milly La Forêt, France

■

NAT "KING" COLE
1919—1965

With a voice like velvet and a piano style to match, he became the first African American to have his own national radio and television shows (with the latter banned in the South). NBC, in an unprecedented departure from their usual practices, carried his TV show without commercial sponsors, a decision that prompted Cole to utter his unforgettable remark, "Madison Avenue is afraid of the dark." As the first black man to tour the United States with an integrated ensemble, he became an American superstar singing songs like "Mona Lisa" and "Ballerina," performing for President John F. Kennedy and being presented to Queen Elizabeth II at a command performance. In spite of his vast popularity he spent his life as a victim of racial prejudice in a country that wanted his talent but not his presence as a neighbor; his home in Los Angeles was vandalized repeatedly.

BURIED: Forest Lawn, Glendale, California

■

COLETTE
1873—1954

The French author of *Gigi* became a cult figure for her writing and her life-style, both of which centered around sensual pleasures. Her early work was published under her husband's name, Henry Gauthier-Villars, a man who locked Colette in her room and forced her to produce novels. She was the first woman in France ever accorded a state funeral.

BURIED: Père Lachaise Cemetery, Paris, France

■

JOHN COLTRANE
1926—1967

"Trane" extended the expressive power of the saxophone by creating a highly original sound that expressed his intense spirituality. In so doing, he changed the direction and sound of American jazz perhaps more than any other musician of his generation.

BURIED: Pinelawn Cemetery, Farmingdale, Long Island, New York

■

CHRISTOPHER COLUMBUS
1451—1506

Erroneously known as "the man who discovered America," he was an Italian maritime explorer who worked for the king and queen of Spain. In search of a cheaper and quicker way to India, he set sail traveling west across the Atlantic and landed somewhere in the Bahamas. He returned several times to explore (and exploit) the South American continent, bringing with him shiploads of convicted criminals who proceeded to destroy the native populations. He fell into disgrace and was returned to Spain where he died in complete obscurity as a prisoner in chains.

BURIED: Seville Cathedral, Seville, Spain

∎

COMANCHE

This horse was the sole survivor of Custer's forces in the battle at Little Bighorn.

STUFFED: On display in Dyche Hall, University of Kansas, Museum of Natural History, Lawrence, Kansas

∎

JACKIE COOGAN
1914–1984

As the costar of *The Kid* with Charlie Chaplin, he was forever instilled in the minds of America as a "child star," and his career as an adult never quite lived up to expectations. Because his parents squandered the fortune he made as a child, the "Coogan Law" was passed in order to protect future children from financial abuse. He was married for a time to Betty Grable, and after their divorce she became a star, while his career faded.

BURIED: Holy Cross Cemetery, Culver City, California

■

TERENCE CARDINAL COOKE
1921–1983

As the secretary of Francis Cardinal Spellman, he clawed his way up the ecclesiastical ladder to become the archbishop of New York. Like his former boss and "sponsor," he was an archconservative and became one of the most strident voices against abortion that the city and the country has ever known.

BURIED: St. Patrick's Cathedral, New York, New York

■

LOU COSTELLO
1906—1959

The fat half of Abbott & Costello, this funnyman from Paterson, New Jersey, always got the short end of the stick. Along with his fast-talking partner Bud he made dozens of films with titles like *Abbott and Costello Go to Mars* (or *to Alaska*) and *Abbott and Costello Meet the Killers* (or *Frankenstein*). The duo tried their comedic skills on television for one year, but the show was a flop.

BURIED: Calvary Cemetery, Los Angeles, California

■

SIR NOEL COWARD
1899—1973

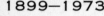

Author of twenty-seven plays, over two hundred and fifty songs, various revues, sketches, musical comedies, and operettas, each one filled with urbane sophistication, he was one of the most versatile artists of the modern age. Among his most successful stage hits are *Blithe Spirit*, *Design for Living*, and *Private Lives*. Credited as an actor, writer, producer, and director, his many films include the classic *Brief Encounter*. In spite of his enormous success, there were years when his work fell out of favor (due in part to his leaving England for tax purposes), but in 1966, when he wrote the autobiographical drama *Song at Twilight*, interest in his work was revived. Best friends with the Queen Mother, he was not knighted until very near his death, apparently because of the royal family's discomfort with his obvious sexual preference for men.

BURIED: Firefly Hill, Grantstown, Jamaica

■

WALLY COX
1924—1973

This milquetoastlike man was the star of the long-running 1950s television show "Mr. Peepers" and was an early roommate and close friend of the young Marlon Brando.

CREMATED: Ashes scattered at sea, Provincetown, Massachusetts

■

JOAN CRAWFORD
1904—1977

This Hollywood star won an Oscar playing the role of a domineering mother and successful businesswoman in *Mildred Pierce*, a part she undoubtedly found easy to portray. In reality she was an obsessive-compulsive who virtually tortured her children, a racist who once

ripped out the tiles in her bathroom after finding a strand of hair she believed belonged to her black maid, and a ruthless career-woman who rose from silent stag films to be for a time one of the queens of Hollywood. She never retired gracefully from films, however, and her last movie was a grade-B flick called *Trog* by the studios and a sad joke by the public. She died from cancer after refusing treatment because of her newly found Christian Science faith.

BURIED: Ferncliff Mausoleum, Hartsdale, New York

∎

JIM CROCE
1943–1973

At the age of twenty-six he released his first album, which failed miserably. Three years later, his second album reached the Top Ten with hits like "You Don't Mess Around With Jim," "Operator," and "Bad Bad Leroy Brown." During a tour across America his plane crashed in Louisiana, ending his life but not his popularity. "I'll Have to Say I Love You in a Song" was released posthumously, becoming his biggest hit and a modern classic.

BURIED: Haym Salomon Memorial Park, Frazer, Pennsylvania

∎

BING CROSBY
1904—1977

To millions of adoring fans he was the crooner who sang "White Christmas." Appearing easygoing, kind and gentlemanly, his early career was almost scuttled because of alcohol abuse. His first wife, Dixie Lee, dragged him back to sobriety, only to be ignored by him when she lay on her deathbed dying of cancer. His screen image was protected by the studios, and he was nothing like the priest he played in *Going My Way*, a role that brought him an Oscar. Allegedly mean and dictatorial to his children, this much-loved singer, who died on a golf course, seemed little more than a bully with a pleasant voice.

BURIED: Holy Cross Cemetery, Culver City, California

■

e e cummings
1894—1962

The American poet, who experimented with language and punctuation in his work, was also an accomplished visual painter. His autobiographical prose work, *The Enormous Room*, is an account of his internment in a French concentration camp during World War I and is considered a definitive portrait of that war.

BURIED: Forest Hills Cemetery, Boston, Massachusetts

■

JACKIE CURTIS
1947—1985

Christened John Holder at birth, the irrepressible playwright and actor lit up the Off-Off Broadway stages with his female persona, Jackie Curtis, in such romps as *Vicissitudes of the Damned, Vain Victory,* Heaven Grand in *Amber Orbit,* and *Glamour, Glory, and Gold.* He also appeared in Andy Warhol's film *Women in Revolt* opposite Candy Darling and Holly Woodlawn, completing the transvestite triumvirate. His last film role was that of the nurse in William Burroughs's *Naked Lunch.* Dressed in a tux in his coffin after he died of a drug overdose, his body was surrounded by heaps of bouquets and showered with glitter, and the coffin was filled with gifts brought by those in attendance.

BURIED: Rose Hill Cemetery, Putnam Valley, New York

GEORGE CUSTER
1839—1876

A graduate of West Point, he fought in the Civil War as the youngest general of the Union forces, battled Southern troops at Gettysburg, and received the Confederate flag of surrender at Appomattox. Court-martialed once, he was reinstated and later accused of abandoning his men in the war against the Indians.

Most famous for his fatal blunder at the battle of Little Bighorn, he was killed along with every single member of his two-hundred-man militia after being overwhelmed by the Sioux. His men were buried at the site of the battle, but Custer's body was interred at his alma mater over the opposition of those who thought him a total incompetent.

BURIED: West Point Cemetery, U.S. Military Academy, West Point, New York

∎

RICHARD J. DALEY
1902—1976

After losing his first campaign, Daley was appointed by Adlai Stevenson to a post in the Illinois Democratic Party that eventually led to his election as mayor of Chicago. A brilliant politician, he quickly developed the "Daley Machine," a powerful political base that kept him in office for three decades and enabled him to gain credit for the narrow election victory of John F. Kennedy. As the host of the Democratic Convention in 1968, he shocked the nation by unleashing his thuglike cops on peaceful demonstrators outside the convention hall. The bloody riots were covered live on national television, making the mayor a hero to some viewers and a monster to others.

BURIED: Holy Sepulchre Cemetery, Worth, Illinois

∎

SALVADOR DALI
1904—1989

Dali's knack for relentless self-promotion propelled him from being an excellent Spanish surrealist painter into a media celebrity and a clown. A precursor to Warhol, he signed napkins, flesh, and blank pieces of paper. He was more famous for his fractured English, elaborate moustache, and the bizarre statements he made as a frequent guest on television talk shows than for his talent, which diminished with age. He spent his last years completely senile, living as a virtual prisoner in his beloved Spain, signing sheets of blank paper that were then turned into "original" Dali prints for what had become an international scam and a small industry.

BURIED: Inner Courtyard, The Theater-Museum Dali, Figueras, Spain

■

DOROTHY DANDRIDGE
1922—1965

After starting in films as a child, this beautiful African-American actress became the female counterpart to Harry Belafonte (both were light-skinned enough for white audiences to accept), with whom she starred in *Carmen Jones* and *Island in the Sun*. After appearing in the Hollywood version of *Porgy and Bess*, the unhappy star ended her troubled life with an overdose of pills prescribed for chronic depression.

BURIED: Forest Lawn, Glendale, California

■

BOBBY DARIN
1936—1973

He began his rise to stardom with two enormous hit songs, "Queen of the Hop" and "Splish Splash," before writing the rock classic "Dream Lover." After the British invasion, he no longer seemed right for the role of a rocker, and he assumed the stance of a new Frank Sinatra, releasing "Mack the Knife," which hit the top of the national charts. He won an Oscar nomination for his role in the movie *Captain Newman, M.D.* and died of a heart attack at the age of thirty-seven.

BODY DONATED TO SCIENCE

■

CANDY DARLING
1945—1974

Named John by his parents, Candy always knew he was destined for stardom as one of the most flamboyant drag queens ever to hit the New York City streets.

Tall, leggy, and platinum blonde, he modeled his female persona on a combination of Marilyn Monroe and Kim Novak and was a well-known barfly and disco diva before appearing on the silver screen in Andy Warhol's *Women in Revolt*. While he was on his deathbed, slowly dying of disease, Peter Hujar took the famous photo of Candy in full makeup reclining in bed and holding a single rose. It remains an unforgettable image of self-creation. At the funeral he was dressed in a pink gown designed by Giorgio di Sant'Angelo, and two mementos were offered to the mourners, one for the fabulous Candy Darling and the other for John.

CREMATED: Ashes remain with his parents, Massapequa, New York

■

CHARLES DARWIN
1809—1882

The English naturalist, who first abandoned careers in both medicine and religion, spent five years aboard the ship *Beagle* observing, recording, and formulating his theory of organic evolution. He then spent the rest of his life writing about his discoveries and perfecting his theories in *The Origin of Species* and *The Descent of Man*.

BURIED: Westminster Abbey, London, England

■

BETTE DAVIS
1908—1989

A true Hollywood legend, Davis spent her entire adult
life making movies. She survived several bouts of "box
office poison" only to climb even higher into the rare-
fied air of superstardom. By her own admission her
favorite film was *Dark Victory*, but her legions of fans
have their own favorites, with *Now Voyager* and *All
About Eve* two of the most popular choices. Always
bigger than life, she was indomitable until the end of
her life, an inspiration both on- and offscreen. In her
last years she was saddened by her daughter, who
became a born-again Christian and then wrote an unflattering book about her famous mother.

BURIED: Forest Lawn, Glendale, California

■

SAMMY DAVIS, JR.
1925—1990

Nicknamed "Mr. Entertainment," the multitalented
entertainer started performing at the age of three and
didn't quit until he died of cancer. With his hair
straightened, and wearing enough rings and jewelry
to make Liberace blink, he danced, he acted, he sang,
he converted to Judaism, and he even hugged Richard
M. Nixon on television—a sight that caused shudders
in the African-American community. He would do anything to be loved by the public, and his death brought

him the accolades and tributes that he relentlessly strived for.

BURIED: Forest Lawn, Glendale, California

■

JAMES DEAN
1931—1955

This bad-boy actor had made only three films, *East of Eden, Giant,* and *Rebel Without a Cause,* when he was killed in a car crash at the age of twenty-four. Allegedly nicknamed the "human ashtray" because of his somewhat bizarre sexual habits, he was a complicated, shy, narcissistic young man who, simply by dying young and in a car, seemed to fill a vacant space in the pantheon of adolescent heroes. Almost forty years after his death, his cult followers are as numerous as ever, the still-growing numbers matched only by those of Elvis Presley's devoted fans.

BURIED: Park Cemetery, Fairmount, Indiana

■

CLAUDE DEBUSSY
1862—1918

The French composer abandoned standard musical forms in works like *La Mer* and *Prélude à L'Après-*

84

midi d'un faune in order to create music that is often called impressionistic. Some of the world's most beautiful music was written by this grossly overweight man who, despite his grotesque appearance, had a fatal charm; two of his ex-girlfriends shot themselves in despair when he discarded them for a wealthy woman.

BURIED: Passy Cemetery, Paris, France

∎

EDGAR DEGAS
1834—1917

Allied with the impressionists, Degas differed from his contemporaries by completing his canvases indoors, not outdoors directly from nature, as the others did. His favorite haunts were the ballet stages, the cafés, and the racetracks of Paris. Working from sketches he had done away from his studio, he created compositions that, influenced by photography and Japanese block prints, were uniquely off-center and immediate. Abandoning oil paint due to his failing eyesight, he turned to pastels, charcoal, and sculpture. The lover of Mary Cassatt and a mean-spirited misogynist, Degas is one of the world's most beloved artists.

BURIED: Montmartre Cemetery, Paris, France

∎

CECIL B. DeMILLE
1881–1959

This was the man who founded Hollywood in a barn. After being sent west by Sam Goldwyn to scout for shooting locations and finding nothing in Colorado, he kept going and settled in Los Angeles. Famous for both his films and dictatorial presence on the set, he was the master of the "epic" and originated the phrase "a cast of thousands" in such films as *The Ten Commandments, King of Kings*, and *The Greatest Show on Earth*.

BURIED: Hollywood Memorial Park, Los Angeles, California

■

ALBERT DE SALVO
1931–1973

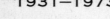

After allegedly confessing to a court-appointed psychiatrist that he was the "Boston Strangler," he was incarcerated to await trial for the murders of thirteen women. The question of his guilt became moot after he was stabbed to death by his fellow inmates.

BURIED: Puritan Lawn Cemetery, Peabody, Massachusetts

■

SERGEI DIAGHILEV
1872—1929

The Russian-born ballet impresario moved to Paris
and established the Ballet Russe, a company that revolutionized the dance world. Determined to integrate
choreography, music and scenic design, he commis-
sioned work from Stravinsky and Picasso. Brilliant,
imposing, and tyrannical, he fired the great dancer
Nijinsky after the young man left him for a woman.

BURIED: Isola de San Michele, Venice, Italy

CHARLES DICKENS
1812—1870

A success at the age of twenty-five, Dickens went on
to become one of the most productive English writers
of the Victorian era, writing such classics as *A Tale
of Two Cities*, *David Copperfield*, and *A Christmas
Carol*. He had a happy marriage, a large family, and
a vast circle of friends, when he met the young actress
Ellen Ternan in 1858; the ensuing scandal led to a
separation from his wife. He died suddenly while on
tour reading from his own work.

BURIED: Poet's Corner, Westminster Abbey, London,
England

EMILY DICKINSON
1830—1886

Only seven out of the two thousand poems she wrote
were published in her own lifetime, and these appeared
anonymously. In twenty years, Dickinson went from
being a witty, outgoing young girl to a total recluse,
refusing even to leave her house in Amherst. Her work
began to appear four years after her death, and at first
she was considered an eccentric minor poet. Her reputation grew slowly until she at last gained her proper
stature as one of America's most startling poetic
voices.

BURIED: West Cemetery, Amherst, Massachusetts

JOHN DILLINGER
1902—1934

He was Public Enemy Number One, gunned down by
the Chicago police after being betrayed by the mysterious "Lady in Red." Contrary to popular myth his
allegedly foot-long penis is definitely not on exhibit at
the Smithsonian Institution.

BURIED: Crown Hill Cemetery, Indianapolis, Indiana

WALT DISNEY
1901–1966

Who would have thought that the man who created Mickey Mouse and *Snow White and the Seven Dwarfs* would also be responsible for forming a right-wing hate group (along with his pals, Ronald Reagan, Adolph Menjou, Hedda Hopper, and Ward Bond) in order to consolidate his power in Hollywood? Using the threat of communism as an excuse, the group was formed in an attempt to foster anti-Semitism and gain control of the studios from the powers that be. His virulent anti-Semitism aside, he did manage to create miracles of color and animation with films like *Pinocchio*, *Bambi*, *Fantasia*, and *Dumbo* and to build the biggest theme park in the world, Disneyland.

BURIED: Forest Lawn, Glendale, California

■

FATHER DIVINE
1877–1965

His real name was George Baker, and he was a southern preacher who moved to New York, where he found fame and fortune. A charismatic cult leader, he advocated the renunciation of private property (his followers donated their possessions to the organization and embraced communal living) and a strict moral code of no alcohol, sex, drugs, or cigarettes. His followers, seventy-five percent of them African Americans and twenty-five percent Caucasians, dispersed after his death.

BURIED: Woodmont Palace Mission Estate, Gladwine, Pennsylvania

∎

LORD ALFRED DOUGLAS
1873—1945

Known as "Bosie" to his friends, Lord Douglas was the alleged lover of Oscar Wilde and the young man who inadvertently caused the downfall of the great Irish playwright. Son of the Marquess of Queensberry, Bosie challenged his father's written denunciation of Wilde, a charge that included the then-illegal act of sodomy. Spurred on by the young lord, Wilde sued the marquess for defamation and lost, a judgment that sent Wilde to prison.

BURIED: Franciscan Friary Cemetery, Crawley, Sussex, England

∎

FREDERICK DOUGLASS
1817—1895

As the most important and powerful African American during the Civil War, he became the conscience of the

nation with his determination to help abolish slavery. Son of a white man and a black woman, and born into slavery, he exhorted President Lincoln to emancipate the slaves and to let them serve in the Union Army so that The War Between the States might be waged for a higher purpose. His contributions to the history of black America rank alongside those of the Reverend Martin Luther King, Jr.

BURIED: Mt. Hope Cemetery, Rochester, New York

■

W.E.B. DU BOIS
1868—1963

After earning his Ph.D. at Harvard, this African-American writer, scholar, and civil-rights activist spent his life fighting for his people. He helped found the NAACP in 1910, edited the organization's magazine *The Crisis*, and established the Niagara Movement, a group that called for immediate implementation of civil rights. Twenty years before his death, he was the first black man admitted to the National Institute of Arts and Letters. In 1961 he joined the Communist Party and moved to Ghana.

BURIED: Government House Cemetery, Accra, Ghana

■

MARGARET DUMONT
1889—1965

As "straight woman" to the Marx brothers, both on stage (in *Cocoanuts*) and in film (*A Night at the Opera*), she never knew what was going to happen next, since scripts were often abandoned in favor of improvisation. Always the butt of their jokes, Dumont remained a lady by carrying herself with regal aplomb.

BURIED: Chapel of the Pines, Los Angeles, California

■

ISADORA DUNCAN
1878—1927

The expatriated American dancer found fame in Europe and Russia as both a performer and teacher of dance. Her unorthodox methods shocked her audiences not only because of the way she danced (barefoot) but also due to the politics her work openly espoused (socialism). She moved from Europe to South America and later to Moscow, where she married a Russian poet who killed himself. Both her children died in an automobile accident, and she herself was strangled by her own scarf after it became tangled in the wheel of a sports car in which she was riding. Her life was the subject of a masterful film called *Isadora* starring Vanessa Redgrave.

BURIED: Père Lachaise Cemetery, Paris, France

■

DOMINIQUE DUNNE
1959—1982

This pretty young film actress, who had a supporting role in the immensely successful film *Poltergeist*, was murdered by her boyfriend, a jealous and abusive man, who strangled her to death in her own driveway. Her father, author Dominick Dunne, wrote a chilling account of the trial, citing the judge's incompetence in letting the killer off with a very light sentence and in refusing to allow testimony that the man had allegedly tried to kill several of his former girlfriends.

BURIED: Westwood Village Memorial Park, Los Angeles, California

■

WILL DURANT
1885—1981

ARIEL DURANT
1898—1981

The husband-and-wife historians, who wrote *The Story of Civilization*, a multivolume overview of man's accomplishments and failures, both died in the same year, ending their legendary sixty-eight-year love affair with history and each other.

BURIED: Westwood Memorial Park, Los Angeles, California

■

JIMMY DURANTE
1893—1980

The American comedian, whose fame rested upon his enormous nose, was nicknamed The Schnozzola. He moved from vaudeville into films, mostly Hollywood musicals like *You're in the Army Now* or comedies like *It's a Mad Mad Mad Mad World*. He almost stole the show away from Monty Woolley in *The Man Who Came to Dinner*, playing a reporter named Banjo, a character modeled after the wacky Harpo Marx. Adored by his fans, he always ended his television show with the mysterious and bittersweet, "Good night, Mrs. Calabash, wherever you are."

BURIED: Holy Cross Cemetery, Culver City, California

■

THOMAS EAKINS
1844—1916

Considered one of the foremost portrait painters in America's history, he was also a photographer, inventor, and sculptor. During his tenure at the Philadelphia Academy of Fine Arts he shocked the patrons with his unflattering realism and was dismissed for using nude male models. Eakins was a scientific artist dedicated to depicting reality; therefore, most of his canvases were too graphic for his day. His work was largely ignored while he was still alive, but he is now hailed as an American master.

BURIED: Woodlands Cemetery, Philadelphia, Pennsylvania

MARY BAKER EDDY
1821–1910

The lady who founded the Christian Science Church spent most of her early life plagued with a series of illnesses. Thinking that she had cured herself by studying the Bible and using her own mind, she published *Science and Health*, laying down the doctrine of her church. Married three times, she made it clear to her followers that illness was a state of mind to be cured with prayer and not with medicine or doctors. Her practices are still followed to this day, often jeopardizing children whose parents frequently face subsequent criminal charges.

BURIED: Mt. Auburn Cemetery, Cambridge, Massachusetts

NELSON EDDY
1901–1967

America loved to hear this photogenic baritone croon in films like *Naughty Marietta*, *Rose Marie*, and *Maytime*, but the critics covered their ears.

BURIED: Hollywood Memorial Park Cemetery, Los Angeles, California

THOMAS ALVA EDISON
1847—1931

The inventor of the light bulb, the microphone, the phonograph, and the motion picture camera was actually a ruthless businessman interested in the practical and commercial applications of his inventions. It is believed by many that in his zeal to gain the patent rights to the first motion picture camera, he arranged the murder of its original French inventor.

BURIED: Edison National Historic Site, West Orange, New Jersey

ETHYL EICHELBERGER
1945—1990

The actor and performance artist, who committed suicide by slashing his wrists after learning he had AIDS, began his career as a wigmaker for Charles Ludlam's Theatre of the Ridiculous. Famous in New York City for playing both male and female roles in his one-person shows, his creations included Medusa, both Abraham and Mary Todd Lincoln, and "Ariadne Obnoxious" on rollerskates. In his adaptation of *King Lear* (which he entitled *Leer*), he played the king, the fool, and Cordelia while accompanying himself on accordion, piano, and concertina. As a circus artist with the Flying Karamazov Brothers, he did cartwheels and ate fire. Born to Amish parents and named James Roy

at birth, Eichelberger was cast as himself in Oliver
Stone's film about Jim Morrison and The Doors.

CREMATED: Ashes interred at St. John the Divine Cathedral, New York, New York

■

ALBERT EINSTEIN
1879—1955

With his wild, white hair and appearance of absent-
mindedness, Einstein is generally seen as the archetypal scientist and the smartest man of the twentieth
century. He was actually a simple and kind man im-
pervious to his own fame and without ambition. The
magnitude of his achievements and the profundity of
his ideas belied this gentle man, who once said, "God
does not play dice." Although a pacifist, he urged President Roosevelt to develop the atom bomb, and he was
a supporter of Zionism.

CREMATED: Ashes scattered in the Delaware River,
Trenton, New Jersey

■

SERGEI EISENSTEIN
1898—1948

The Russian director was responsible for the silent
film classics *Potemkin* and *Ten Days That Shook the*

World. His first talkie, *Alexander Nevsky*, made him an international star whose extensive writings on the art of the cinema continue to influence filmmakers.

BURIED: Novo Devich Cemetery, Moscow, USSR

■

GEORGE ELIOT
1819—1880

Born Mary Ann Evans, the English novelist was a free-thinking radical who renounced all religion and had an open "marriage" with G. H. Lewes (who was separated from his wife) that lasted until his death. Praised by Dickens for her prose, Eliot wrote *Silas Marner*, a book that brought her great success. By the time she produced her masterpiece, *Middlemarch*, she was considered the greatest novelist of her day.

BURIED: Highgate Cemetery, London, England

■

T. S. ELIOT
1888—1965

The American expatriate from Missouri, who not only lived in England but also became so English that he once told an American audience that he was a stranger to their country, is considered by many to be the greatest of the modern poets. His last book of poems, *The Four Quartets*, is a masterpiece of intellect and verse, and his plays, *The Cocktail Party* and *Murder in the Cathedral*, are classic works of theater. Edmund Wilson called Eliot "a completely self-invented character." He worked for many years as clerk in an English bank and then as an editor at Faber and Faber. An unhappy marriage caused him much suffering and guilt, which led him into the comforting arms of the Church of England. His religious affiliations eventually pushed him into anti-Semitism and a prudishness that betrayed his keen intelligence and sensitivity.

BURIED: St. Michael's Church, East Coker, England

■

DUKE ELLINGTON
1899—1974

Cotton Club bandleader and composer of such classics as "Mood Indigo," "Don't Get Around Much Anymore," and "Solitude," he became the epitome of Café Society and urban black sophistication. His musical legacy is considered one of America's greatest cultural treasures.

BURIED: Woodlawn Cemetery, Bronx, New York

■

"MAMA" CASS ELLIOT
1941—1974

The hefty lead singer of The Mamas and The Papas forged a brief but successful career of her own after the group disbanded. Usually dressed in flowing, flowery granny dresses, her long hair winding through the love beads she wore, she sang in a powerful and unmistakable voice that helped define the sound of the sixties in such songs as "California Dreaming" and "Monday Monday." Her life came to an abrupt end when she choked on a ham sandwich.

CREMATED: Ashes scattered over the Pacific Ocean

■

MEDGAR EVERS
1925—1963

Murdered just hours after President Kennedy spoke to the nation in an historic civil rights speech, Medgar Evers became a martyr to the civil rights movement. His brother and ally, Charles, carried on the struggle.

BURIED: Arlington National Cemetery, Arlington, Virginia

■

FALA

He was Franklin Delano Roosevelt's little scottie dog, who caused a political uproar and helped the Democratic president get reelected. On a visit to the Pacific during World War II, FDR had brought his dog along for the long ordeal of visiting the troops. When the president returned to Washington, Republicans, desperate to win back the White House, started a rumor that Fala had been inadvertently left behind on a Pacific atoll and had had to be rescued by sending a destroyer at the taxpayers' expense. Roosevelt exposed the story as a lie on one of his radio "fireside chats" to the nation, embarrassing the Republicans and gaining votes in the process.

BURIED: Roosevelt Library and Museum, Hyde Park, New York

■

FANNIE FARMER
1857—1915

The culinary expert, who because of a disability attended cooking classes and later opened her own school in Boston, is credited with introducing the use of measuring devices in her famous cookbook.

BURIED: Mt. Auburn Cemetery, Cambridge, Massachusetts

■

WILLIAM FAULKNER
1897—1962

A lifelong resident of Oxford, Mississippi, he wrote a series of novels that take place in mythical Yoknapatawpha County. He won the Nobel Prize in 1949, and his novels include *As I Lay Dying*, *The Sound and the Fury*, and *Absalom, Absalom!*

BURIED: St. Peter's Cemetery, Oxford, Mississippi

∎

MARTY FELDMAN
1934—1982

He was the popeyed English comedian who achieved cult status in America by appearing in films like *Silent Movie*. In another Mel Brooks film, *Young Frankenstein*, he played a hunchback whose hump moved mysteriously from side to side.

BURIED: Forest Lawn Hollywood Hills, Los Angeles, California

∎

W. C. FIELDS
1880—1946

Known as Woody to his friends, the unforgettable actor with the bulbous nose became famous for his comic timing and his ability to juggle props gracefully. It was said that he once fell down a full flight of stairs without spilling a drop of his martini. Able to tolerate large quantities of alcohol (although unable to tolerate others' drinking), it is said that he once refused a glass of water because "ducks fuck in water." Famous for both his humor and his stinginess, Fields never owned his own home and had a long-standing affair with the actress Carlotta Monti. His films include *The Dentist, You Can't Cheat an Honest Man* and *My Little Chickadee*; in this last film he was teamed with his comic equal, Mae West.

BURIED: Forest Lawn, Glendale, California

■

PETER FINCH
1916—1977

Finch won an Oscar for his riveting performance in *Network* as a demented news anchor who coined the phrase that swept the U.S., "I'm mad as hell, and I'm not going to take it anymore!" He also played the tortured bisexual in Penelope Gilliatt's masterpiece, *Sunday, Bloody Sunday.*

BURIED: Hollywood Memorial Park Cemetery, Los Angeles, California

■

LARRY FINE
1902—1975

He was the frizzy-haired member of the Three Stooges.

BURIED: Forest Lawn, Glendale, California

■

F. SCOTT FITZGERALD
1896—1940

As the "Voice of the Jazz Age," his first novel, *This Side of Paradise*, made him rich, famous, and respected as a writer. He married the glamorous Zelda Sayre, and they began a fast-paced life together, spending money more quickly than he could make it, and being pursued by creditors across several continents. Zelda eventually broke down and was hospitalized in 1930. His life and career in ruins, Scott resurrected his reputation by publishing *The Great Gatsby*, a portrayal of the spiritual barrenness of the 1920s in America that many consider his finest work. No amount of money and fame could prevent his own eventual breakdown, however, and he spent his final years as a Hollywood scriptwriter and the lover of Sheilah Graham, the gossip columnist.

BURIED: St. Mary's Cemetery, Rockville, Maryland

■

ZELDA FITZGERALD
1900—1948

The multitalented, beautiful, but unstable wife of F. Scott Fitzgerald, she mirrored her husband's self-destructive habits in the "Age of the Flapper." Beginning in 1930, a decade after her marriage, she began what was to become a lifelong series of stays in a sanitorium, during which she wrote a novel, *Save Me the Waltz*, and various short stories. Prone to setting her own hair on fire, she perished when the wing of her hospital burned to the ground.

BURIED: St. Mary's Cemetery, Rockville, Maryland

■

GUSTAVE FLAUBERT
1821—1880

The French novelist shocked the world with his *Madame Bovary*, a tale of lust, infidelity, and of suicide. Some consider this work to be the best novel ever written. Agonizing over every sentence, he looked upon his creative endeavors as "bloodletting" and compared entering his study as being "akin to torture."

BURIED: The churchyard at Canteleu, Rouen, France

■

ERROL FLYNN
1909—1959

Swashbuckling his way through films like *Captain Blood* and mesmerizing an entire generation of children as Robin Hood, he represented the dashing, handsome outcast with a heart of gold. In his private life he was a drug addict, wore flesh-colored latex bathing suits rather than underwear, was prosecuted for sexually abusing young girls, banned from hanging around school playgrounds, and reportedly had a tempestuous love affair with Tyrone Power. The still popular expression "in like Flynn" refers to this star's incredible powers of seduction.

BURIED: Forest Lawn, Glendale, California

■

MALCOLM FORBES
1919—1990

The American millionaire publisher of *Forbes* magazine was famous for throwing lavish parties for the world's elite. Dressed in leather from head to toe and straddling his motorcycle, he spent his evenings visiting the waterfront gay bars in New York City. Forbes used his family and his friendships with some of the world's most beautiful women (Liz Taylor, among others) to remain closeted. In one of the most shameful displays of his wealth he invited hundreds of celebrities to North Africa to celebrate what was to be his last birthday. His guests consumed millions of dollars worth of gourmet food and wine on a continent where thousands were dying of starvation every day. It is rumored that he took his own life after learning he was dying of AIDS.

CREMATED: Ashes scattered off the island of Fiji

■

JOHN FORD
1895—1973

Born in Maine, he thrilled several generations world-wide with his epic westerns, putting his indelible stamp on the genre as no one had before or has since. He had over two hundred films to his credit and won Oscars for *The Grapes of Wrath*, *How Green Was My Valley*, and *The Quiet Man*.

BURIED: Holy Cross Cemetery, Culver City, California

■

E. M. FORSTER
1879—1970

As the author of such modern classics as *A Room With a View*, *A Passage to India*, and *Howards End*, Morgan (as he was called by his friends) spent most of his adult life quietly teaching at Cambridge University in England. His homosexuality was revealed finally with the posthumous publication of *Maurice*, a book he had written but suppressed during his own lifetime. A shy and serious thinker, he was adored by his students and friends, telling those closest to him that he wanted his ashes scattered wherever he happened to be at the time of his death. His wishes were honored.

CREMATED: Ashes scattered, Coventry, England

■

WILLIAM FRAWLEY
1887—1966

Gruff and potbellied, Frawley played the part of Fred Mertz, landlord to the Ricardos on *I Love Lucy*. He was a problem drinker but never missed a shooting— or a chance to insult his on-screen wife, Vivian Vance, whom he hated.

BURIED: San Fernando Mission Cemetery, Los Angeles, California

■

SIGMUND FREUD
1856—1939

The father of psychoanalysis collected mushrooms and used cocaine briefly on himself and his patients as a cure for fatigue. His work, including the masterwork *The Interpretation of Dreams*, changed the course of medicine forever and opened the door to an entirely new way of dealing with mental illness, although recent discoveries in biochemistry have called into question many of his original theories and methods of treating schizophrenia and manic depression. His obsession with childhood sexuality strikes many modern thinkers as ill-conceived and perhaps a reflection of his own neuroses. Trapped inside Austria during the Nazi occupation, he was forced to make a pro-Nazi statement before being allowed to emigrate to England, and he did so with as much cynicism as he could muster. After thirty-three operations for cancer, he endured great pain each day without the help of drugs.

CREMATED: Ashes stored in his favorite Grecian urn, Golders Green, London, England

■

ROBERT FROST
1874—1963

The California-born poet moved to New England and spent his life having a "lover's quarrel with the world." Unhappy and broke at the age of forty, he gave up his

professions as farmer and shoemaker, moved to England, and started writing poetry under the tutelage of Ezra Pound. An early collection of his poems, *North of Boston*, became a best-seller, and he toured the country as a performer of his poems, rather like Rod McKuen. He was the first Poet-in-Residence at Amherst College and won four Pulitzer Prizes. Frost read at the inauguration of John F. Kennedy, making him the first poet to speak on such an occasion. His personal life was filled with tragedy, and he was rumored to be a terrible husband and an even worse father to his children. In spite of his bucolic verse and his enormous popularity, he was dubbed the "Poet of Terror."

BURIED: Old Bennington Cemetery, Bennington, Vermont

BUCKMINSTER FULLER
1895—1983

A born environmentalist, "Bucky's" entire life was dedicated to experimenting with the most efficient use of the world's natural resources. His inventions include the geodesic dome and a shower that allowed the bather a ten-minute rinse but used only one quart of water.

BURIED: Mt. Auburn Cemetery, Cambridge, Massachusetts

CLARK GABLE
1901—1960

At the peak of his career he was an American sex symbol, the male equivalent of Marilyn Monroe. When he appeared without an undershirt in *It Happened One Night* with Claudette Colbert, millions of men across the country stopped wearing undershirts, and sales plummeted; his fans would do anything to copy his style. Married five times, twice to older women, his most famous wife was Carole Lombard, who died young in a plane crash. Early in his career he was chosen by Garbo to play her leading man in *Susan Lenox: Her Fall and Rise*, the only film they made together. His most famous role was that of Rhett Butler, the scallywag who marries Scarlett O'Hara in *Gone With the Wind*, probably the most famous film ever made. Just before his death, he completed work on Arthur Miller's *The Misfits*, costarring Montgomery Clift and Marilyn Monroe, both of whom were to die within the next few years.

BURIED: Forest Lawn, Glendale, California

■

JOEY GALLO
1929—1972

Gallo was a high-level gangster, a member of the mob, and the destroyer of Joe Columbo. He lived a glamorous life hobnobbing with New York's theatrical elite until he was gunned down in a Little Italy clam house.

He was later immortalized as a folk hero in a very long song by Bob Dylan called "Joey."

BURIED: Green-Wood Cemetery, Brooklyn, New York

∎

MOHANDAS K. GANDHI
1869—1948

The "Father of India," he led nonviolent protests of passive resistance that brought independence to his country. A successful barrister educated in England, he began his struggles fighting against apartheid in South Africa. Once back in India, he led the struggle to free his own country from Great Britain's oppressive rule, and was given the title Mahatma, meaning "great-souled," by his followers. Dedicated to non-violence, he was never able to stem the racial and religious hatred within the subcontinent and was killed by an assassin's bullet.

CREMATED: Ashes scattered on the Ganges River, Benares, India

∎

AVA GARDNER
1922—1990

The "Barefoot Contessa," whose sultry sexuality on the screen propelled her to stardom for most of her

adult life, had a penchant for bullfighters and was always the first to admit she was not a great actress. Her early years were filled with marriage and divorce, with Frank Sinatra and Mickey Rooney among her husbands. Her later years were spent as an expatriate in Europe, finally settling in England, where she died.

BURIED: Sunset Memorial Park, Smithfield, North Carolina

■

JOHN GARFIELD
1913–1952

Rumored to have died from a heart attack in the midst of copulation at the age of thirty-nine, he is best remembered for playing Lana Turner's lover in *The Postman Always Rings Twice*.

BURIED: Westchester Hills Cemetery, Hastings-on-Hudson, New York

■

JUDY GARLAND
1922–1969

One of the towering geniuses of stage and screen, Judy spent her entire life before the public. Battered and abused by her mother and later by Louis B. Mayer (who was responsible for her addiction to drugs as a

teenager), she was never able to recover fully. One of the first major child stars in the Andy Hardy series, her career spanned decades, from *The Wizard of Oz* through *A Star Is Born* to *Judgment at Nuremberg*. Although delicate and frail, her live performances showcased her powerful personality and unforgettable voice. She left a legacy of recordings that include *Judy: Live at Carnegie Hall*, and in the 1960s she had her own short-lived television show, on which she generously introduced future stars like her daughter, Liza Minnelli, and Barbra Streisand.

BURIED: Ferncliff Mausoleum, Hartsdale, New York

■

PAUL GAUGUIN
1848—1903

The French artist started his career as a stockbroker in Paris, painting on the weekends, when suddenly at the age of thirty-five he left his job, his wife, and his five children in order to devote himself to painting full-time. Sick of civilization, he traveled to the Caribbean but returned to Europe because of illness. After a brief stay in the South of France, living in Arles with Vincent Van Gogh, he had a violent quarrel with Van Gogh and returned to Paris. With money he made from an exhibition of his work he traveled to Tahiti, where he spent two years painting some of his best work. He revived the art of woodblock prints, wrote an autobiographical novel called *Noa Noa* and lived the life of a "primitive." Returning one last time to France, Gauguin collected a small inheritance and then sailed back to Tahiti, where he spent the rest of his life in poverty, fighting an advanced case of syphilis, warding off recurrent depression—he attempted suicide—and

114

creating some of the most glorious paintings of the twentieth century.

BURIED: Catholic Cemetery, Hueakihi Hill, Atuona, Tahiti

■

JANET GAYNOR
1906—1984

This is the woman who won the very first Academy Award for Best Actress in the film *Seventh Heaven*, a melodrama served to an audience that wanted nothing more than an escape from reality. After marrying Hollywood's best-loved dress designer, Adrian, she faded from the silver screen. She died sitting next to her friend, Mary Martin, after their taxi crashed on the streets of San Francisco.

BURIED: Hollywood Memorial Park Cemetery, Los Angeles, California

■

LOU GEHRIG
1903—1941

The "Pride of the Yankees," Gehrig developed amyotrophic lateral sclerosis (now called "Lou Gehrig's disease") and died at the age of thirty-eight.

BURIED: Kensico Cemetery, Valhalla, New York

■

GORGEOUS GEORGE
1915—1963

We know his real name was George Wagner, but we will never know the real color of his bleached blond locks. The "Liberace of the Wrestling Ring" thrilled his fans more with style than with sport. He usually lost his matches but always won the crowd with his outrageous theatrics.

BURIED: Valhalla Memorial Park Cemetery, Los Angeles, California

■

GERONIMO
1829—1909

The Indian resistance leader was proclaimed "Chief of the Apaches" by his people, even though such a position was historically filled by reason of heredity. Skilled in both battle and diplomacy, he fought the Americans to the north and the Mexicans to the south and was considered the most dangerous Indian alive, killing hundreds of men single-handed. After the government had conquered the Indian nations, Geronimo marched alongside Teddy Roosevelt during a parade in Washington, stealing the show. He died after getting drunk on illegal whiskey and falling off his horse.

BURIED: Apache Cemetery, Fort Sill, Oklahoma

■

GEORGE GERSHWIN
1898—1937

The American composer of *Rhapsody in Blue* and *Porgy and Bess* died of a brain tumor at the age of thirty-eight. He was survived by his brother, Ira (1896–1983), who is buried at the same site.

BURIED: Westchester Hills Cemetery, Hastings-on-Hudson, New York

■

ANDY GIBB
1957—1988

The only Gibb brother who was not a member of the pop rock group The Bee Gees, he had a solo career that included several hits in the Top Forty. He became addicted to drugs, mainly cocaine, and died in England at the age of thirty-one.

BURIED: Forest Lawn, Hollywood Hills, Los Angeles, California

■

GARY GILMORE
1941—1977

Gilmore was the first American executed by the government after the death penalty was reinstated in the United States. His request that his death by firing squad be broadcast on live television was denied.

CREMATED: Ashes scattered over Provo, Utah

■

HERMIONE GINGOLD
1897—1987

This great English actress and comedienne appeared in many dramas and musicals, including *The Pickwick Papers*, *Around the World in 80 Days* and *The Music Man*. As the doting aunt of Leslie Caron in *Gigi*, she lit up the screen in her scenes with Maurice Chevalier, with whom she sang the unforgettable duet, "I Remember It Well."

BURIED: Forest Lawn, Glendale, California

■

GEORGE GIPP
1895—1920

The football player from Notre Dame, who died of pneumonia at the age of twenty-five, lives on forever in the film *Knute Rockne, All American*. The role of the Gipper was played by the actor Ronald Reagan, who, when elected president of the United States, exploited the nickname.

BURIED: Lakeview Cemetery, Laurium, Wisconsin

■

NIKOLAI GOGOL
1809—1852

The Russian playwright and poet was a master of the short story, his genius evident in "The Overcoat" and "The Nose." Unfortunately, he fell under the influence of the Russian Orthodox Church, renounced literature, and burned his manuscripts. Taking the advice of the priests he went on a long fast to purify his soul, which caused his death.

BURIED: Novo Devich Cemetery, Moscow, USSR

■

EMMA GOLDMAN
1869—1940

Born in Russia, this radical Jewish writer moved to America and was sent to prison for urging the unemployed to take the food they needed "by force." Her *Anarchism and Other Essays* is a textbook of revolutionary ideas, including a call for birth control. Deported back to Russia, she joined in the overthrow of the government in 1917 but soon lost interest in the revolution, which resulted in her publishing *My Disillusionment in Russia*. Barred entry into the United States, she lived first in England, then in Canada, where she died. The U.S. government allowed her body back into the country for burial.

BURIED: Waldheim Forest Home Cemetery, Forest Park, Illinois

■

SAMUEL GOLDWYN
1879—1974

Born in Poland, this impresario of the cinema produced some of the finest films ever made and so amassed a fortune. Famous for mangling the English language, he once said, "Anybody who goes to a psychiatrist should have his head examined." And upon introducing Field Marshal Montgomery at an honorary celebration, he called the man "Marshall Field Montgomery." His films include *The Best Years of Our Lives, Meet*

John Doe, and *The Little Foxes* (for which he wangled Bette Davis away from Warner Bros. for the first and only time).

BURIED: Forest Lawn, Glendale, California

■

BETTY GRABLE
1916—1973

The number one pinup girl during World War II, she was the highest-paid woman in America, and her legs were insured by Lloyd's of London for one million dollars. After the boys came home from the war, she remained at the top of her profession for years in such lowbrow musicals as *The Dolly Sisters*. Her marriage to bandleader Harry James was not happy, and her untimely death left a void in the musical comedy world.

BURIED: Inglewood Park Cemetery, Los Angeles, California

■

CARY GRANT
1904—1986

Discovered by Mae West, the debonair film star personified the upper class by looking as comfortable in a tuxedo as he did in tennis shorts. Rumored to have spent his early years in Hollywood closeted in a homosexual liaison with Randolph Scott, he later married several times, always returning to Scott after the divorces. Paired with his class-conscious equal, Katharine Hepburn, in *Bringing Up Baby* and *The Philadelphia Story*, his comic timing was impeccable and a perfect foil for Hepburn's classy hysteria. In a rare departure from its usual protocol, *The New York Times* published a wishful-thinking editorial questioning the reality of his death on the same day it printed his obituary.

CREMATED: Ashes remain with his widow

■

SYDNEY GREENSTREET
1879—1954

It is hard to believe, but this rotund British actor made his film debut at the age of sixty-one in *The Maltese Falcon*. As perfect as he was at being sinister, he could also be charming, as he was in *Christmas in Connecticut* with Barbara Stanwyck, or mysterious, as in *Casablanca* with Bogart and Bergman.

BURIED: Forest Lawn, Glendale, California

■

ZANE GREY
1875—1939

The American writer, who specialized in Westerns and sold over fifteen million copies of his books, is most famous for *Riders of the Purple Sage.*

BURIED: Union Cemetery, Lackawaxen, Pennsylvania

■

D. W. GRIFFITH
1875—1948

He was the man who, more than any other, was responsible for elevating cinema to an art form. After making dozens of forgettable films, he turned his attention to a play called *The Clansman* and turned out an epic he renamed *Birth of a Nation.* This masterpiece of cinematic invention enthralled and angered the American public to such a degree that it became both an artistic triumph and a political hot potato. The NAACP tried to have the film banned, while white sympathizers of the Old South, especially the KKK, saw it as a reason to celebrate. Whatever the film's merits or flaws, it made Lillian Gish an overnight sensation as the embodiment of white purity and caused Griffith's career to soar. He also directed *Intolerance.*

BURIED: Mt. Tabor Methodist Church Graveyard, Crestwood, Kentucky

■

THE BROTHERS GRIMM

JACOB
1785—1863

WILHELM
1786—1859

The authors of *Grimm's Fairy Tales* were philologists and folklorists who were inseparable until the younger Wilhelm's death. After becoming librarians, they began publishing their *Tales*, which in the early nineteenth century became the most widely read book in the world except for the Bible.

BURIED: Matthauskirchoff Cemetery, Berlin, Germany

■

VIRGIL "GUS" GRISSOM
1926—1967

After garnering the distinction of being (in 1961) the third man in space, he was killed on the ground in a simulation of an Apollo I launch.

BURIED: Arlington National Cemetery, Arlington, Virginia

■

PEGGY GUGGENHEIM
1898—1979

A lover of art and artists, this eccentric heiress collected enough modern art to fill her own museum on the Grand Canal in Venice.

BURIED: Salem Fields Cemetery, Brooklyn, New York

■

DR. JOSEPH IGNACE GUILLOTINE
1738—1814

He was the man who invented the device that chopped off people's heads, which the crowds then watched roll into a basket. As it turned out, the crowd got to watch the doctor's head roll as well.

BURIED: Père Lachaise Cemetery, Paris, France

■

WOODY GUTHRIE
1912—1967

Christened Woodrow Wilson Guthrie, he left home at the age of sixteen and wandered across America singing folk songs in bars, pool halls, and dust bowl refugee camps. During this period he wrote such classics as "So Long, It's Been Good to Know You" and "This Land Is Your Land." After quitting his life on the road, he settled in New York City and wrote the story of his life, *Bound for Glory*. The last fifteen years of his life were spent mostly in hospitals suffering from Huntington's disease, which eventually caused his death at the age of fifty-five. He was married three times and had six children, one of whom is the folksinger Arlo Guthrie. His influence on American music is immeasurable; a shining example is his effect on Bob Dylan.

CREMATED: Ashes scattered over the Atlantic Ocean

■

JOAN HACKETT
1942—1983

This talented actress's career was just beginning its ascent when death ended it. While still almost unknown, she starred opposite Charlton Heston in *Will Penny*, a western that might have been easily dismissed and forgotten had it not been for her riveting performance. Her tombstone reads, "Go away! I'm sleeping."

BURIED: Hollywood Memorial Park Cemetery, Los Angeles, California

■

JACK HALEY
1898—1978

After languishing for years in third-rate roles, Jack Haley took over the part of the Tin Man in *The Wizard of Oz* after Buddy Ebsen developed an allergy to the makeup. Decades later he was to become the father-in-law of Judy ("Dorothy") Garland's daughter, Liza Minnelli.

BURIED: Holy Cross Cemetery, Culver City, California

■

RADCLYFFE HALL
1886—1943

The lesbian author of *The Well of Loneliness* was called "John" by her friends. Never one to resist an opportunity to flaunt her sexual preference in public, she often accompanied her beautifully coiffed and regally gowned female lovers to the opera or the theater dressed in a man's tuxedo, with her own hair cut short and parted like a gentleman's. She was one of the most successful lyricists of her time; it was her songs, not her books, that made her a wealthy woman able to indulge her own eccentricities and fantasies to the hilt.

BURIED: Highgate Cemetery, London, England

■

DASHIELL HAMMETT
1894—1961

The inventor of the hard-boiled detective Sam Spade and the author of the American classic *The Maltese Falcon*, "Dash" also created the hard-drinking, debonair couple Nick and Nora Charles in *The Thin Man*. His private life was filled with controversy; he was jailed for his refusal to answer questions from the House Un-American Activities Committee and was the lover of the playwright Lillian Hellman. He suffered years of writer's block. His excessive taste for women and wine defeated him in the end, and Hellman came to his rescue only after repeated prodding from their closest friends and literary alliances, caring for him until he died.

BURIED: Arlington National Cemetery, Arlington, Virginia

■

LORRAINE HANSBERRY
1930—1965

In 1959 the New York Drama Critics Circle Award was given to this talented African-American writer and civil rights activist for her play *A Raisin in the Sun*. Hansberry began her career as an editor and reporter for Paul Robeson's magazine, *Freedom*, and died tragically at the age of thirty-five from cancer while her second play was on Broadway.

BURIED: Beth El Cemetery, Croton-on-Hudson, New York

■

OLIVER HARDY
1892—1957

Known to his friends as "Babe," he was the fat member of the Laurel and Hardy team, the one who always had the answer that, if considered logically, never really made sense. With his moustache and too small bowler hat, he was the epitome of the overweight kid, filled with innocence and optimism, yet stupid enough to fail at everything he tried. The films he made with Stan Laurel, such as *Babes in Toyland* and *Sons of the Desert*, were immensely popular during the Great Depression and are considered classics of the genre.

BURIED: Valhalla Memorial Park, Burbank, California

■

JEAN HARLOW
1911—1937

Discovered by Howard Hughes, she was the original platinum blonde "bombshell," whose comic flair propelled her to stardom for a few short years in films like *Dinner at Eight*. She died at the age of twenty-six from uremic poisoning that might have been treated successfully if her mother's religious beliefs had not prevented medical intervention. An American sex symbol long before Marilyn Monroe, Harlow's real-life husband was impotent, and he killed himself rather than face treatment.

BURIED: Forest Lawn, Glendale, California

BRUNO RICHARD HAUPTMANN
1889—1936

The German-born carpenter was the man convicted of kidnapping and killing the infant son of Charles and Anne Morrow Lindbergh, the famous aviator and his wife. Pleading his innocence until the end, he was sent to the electric chair after a sensational trial that galvanized the nation and altered the laws on kidnapping in the United States.

CREMATED: Ashes scattered in Saxony, Germany

GABBY HAYES
1885—1969

To several generations of children Gabby Hayes was the essence of the Old West in film after film about cowboys. Always a sidekick, this bearded old man added humor and pathos to the genre.

BURIED: Forest Lawn Hollywood Hills, Los Angeles, California

SUSAN HAYWARD
1919—1975

Auburn-haired, sexy, and stunningly beautiful, this actress broke out of the mold Hollywood had created for her by shouting over and over, "I want to live" in the film of the same name, a film that engendered respect for her talent, not just her body.

BURIED: Our Lady's Memorial Garden, Cemetery of Our Lady of Perpetual Help Church, Carrollton, Georgia

RITA HAYWORTH
1918—1987

Born Margarita Cansino of Mexican-American parents, she began her career as a teenager dancing with her father, a man who used and abused her both psychologically and sexually. This pattern of abuse continued with most of the men in her life, including Orson Welles, with whom she had a second daughter. Her marriage to Prince Aly Khan produced her first child, a bona fide princess. Indicted for child neglect while she was married to Dick Haymes, this ravishing red-headed pinup girl danced across the screen with Fred Astaire, shook up the public in *Gilda*, did a ladylike striptease in *Pal Joey*, and spent her last years as a victim of Alzheimer's disease.

BURIED: Holy Cross Cemetery, Culver City, California

■

WILLIAM RANDOLPH HEARST
1863—1951

The immensely successful publisher of both the *San Francisco Examiner* and the *New York Journal*, he built the famous mansion San Simeon for his mistress, Marion Davies, and was the inspiration for *Citizen Kane*, Orson Welles's film masterpiece.

BURIED: Cypress Lawn Cemetery, Colma, California

■

LILLIAN HELLMAN
1905—1984

Her first play, *The Children's Hour*, was an overnight sensation on Broadway. Summoned to Hollywood, she adapted the work to film, eliminating the homosexual relationship in the process, apparently since America was not ready for lesbians on the silver screen. More Broadway successes followed with *Little Foxes* and *Watch on the Rhine*, both box office hits and both made into films. Romantically involved with writer Dashiell Hammett for most of her life, she is famous for telling the House Un-American Activities Committee that she would not "cut her conscience to fit this year's fashion" and was promptly blacklisted. Her writing moved away from the theater, and she devoted several decades to writing what she termed nonfiction and others called lies. Well known for her homely appearance, chain-smoking, and explosive anger, she had many admirers as well as detractors, but her creative work remains a testament to her imagination and talent.

BURIED: Abel's Hill Cemetery, Chilmark, Martha's Vineyard, Massachusetts

ERNEST HEMINGWAY
1899—1961

The American novelist, whose macho stance continues to alienate feminist readers, studied in Paris under Ezra Pound and Gertrude Stein (who coined the phrase "lost generation" to describe Hemingway and his work). After publishing *The Sun Also Rises*, his success was assured. *A Farewell to Arms* followed, along with the short story "The Snows of Kilimanjaro" and his nonfiction account of bullfighting, *Death in the Afternoon*. After serving as a correspondent in the Spanish Civil War, he wrote what some consider his masterpiece, *For Whom the Bell Tolls*. Breaking with Stein (whom some say he loved), he wrote *A Moveable Feast*, in which he lashed out against his former mentor and her lover, Alice B. Toklas. Ill in both mind and body, he returned home and killed himself with a shotgun.

BURIED: Ketchum, Idaho

JIMI HENDRIX
1942—1970

Dressed like a tie-dyed scarecrow, the African-American singer, composer, and guitarist hit the music scene like a bolt of lightning. Made famous by his outrageous stage performances—he would play his guitar with his teeth or set fire to it and then smash it against the speakers—Hendrix is now considered the greatest guitarist of his generation. After his tragic death, hours of unreleased recordings were discovered in his New York recording studio, Electric Lady Land. Released posthumously, this legacy continues to fund a scholarship for young musicians, many of whom visit his grave, which features a marble electric guitar.

BURIED: Greenwood Memorial Park, Renton, Washington

■

SONJA HENIE
1912—1969

The Norwegian figure skater won her first championship at the age of ten, then went on to win gold medals at the Olympics in 1928, 1932, and 1936. After turning pro, she hit Hollywood and starred in a series of blockbuster films like *Second Fiddle* and *Thin Ice* that always included an extravaganza at the rink. She aptly titled her autobiography *Wings on My Feet*.

BURIED: Henie-Onstad Art Center, Oslo, Norway

■

WOODY HERMAN
1913—1987

Woody's first band made their debut at Roseland in Brooklyn, New York; billed as "The Band That Plays the Blues," their big hit was "Woodchopper's Ball." Herman led many bands, calling them "herds," and at New York's Carnegie Hall he premiered *Ebony Concerto*, a composition written for him by Igor Stravinsky.

BURIED: Hollywood Memorial Park, Los Angeles, California

■

HERMANN HESSE
1877—1962

This German writer fled his Nazi-occupied homeland and published his most important work in his adopted Switzerland. *Siddhartha* and *Steppenwolf*, two of his most famous books, became popular in America after sixties guru Timothy Leary called them psychedelic journeys. Often accused of being an elitist, he nonetheless won the Nobel Prize for *The Glass Bead Game*. Hesse spent most of his life fighting off a series of debilitating illnesses and died before his books became worldwide best-sellers.

BURIED: The Cemetery of S. Abbondio, Montagnola, Switzerland

■

CONRAD HILTON
1887—1979

The rags-to-riches industrialist started out as a bell-boy. After moving up the corporate ladder to the top rung, Hilton opened his first hotel, which quickly grew into the worldwide chain of look-alikes that bear his name.

BURIED: Holy Cross Cemetery, Los Angeles, California

ADOLF HITLER
1889—1945

This high-school dropout from Austria lived on charity and by selling hand-painted postcards that he copied from books and paintings. After a brief stint as a housepainter, he moved from Vienna to Munich, joined the German Army, and the rest, as they say, is history. He published *Mein Kampf*, a book that he dictated to Rudolf Hess, and it became, for a while, the German Bible. Near the end of his life, the leader of the Nazi Party confined himself to his bunker in Berlin with his mistress, Eva Braun, after his own men tried to kill him. It was there that he finally married Eva, and one day later they killed themselves in a double suicide—either that or he is alive and well somewhere in South America.

CREMATED: Ashes scattered somewhere in Berlin, Germany

ABBIE HOFFMAN
1937—1989

The absurdist radical, who coined the term *yippie* and published works with unforgettable titles like *Steal This Book* and *Steal This Urine Test* (with Jonathan Silvers), was a political activist who helped alter the landscape of the turbulent 1960s. Arrested often for his commitment to civil disobedience, he went into hiding for many years before resurfacing to continue the struggle for social justice. He was so dismayed by what he perceived as a return to the political right and a reemergence of racism on college campuses that his sense of humor finally failed him, and he committed suicide.

CREMATED: Ashes remain in a jar on top of the television in his former "running mate's" apartment, New York, New York

■

HANS HOFMANN
1880—1966

Born in Germany, this painter was in large part responsible for the emergence of Abstract Expressionism into the forefront of twentieth century art. Both as a teacher (he founded schools in both New York City and Provincetown, Massachusetts) and as a painter, he is credited as being one of the major the-

138

orists of his time, and his work remains on view in most major museums worldwide.

BURIED: Snow Cemetery, Truro, Massachusetts

■

BILLIE HOLIDAY
1915—1959

Widely considered the greatest singer in the history of jazz, she also composed several classics, including "God Bless the Child." She grew up in a bordello, was raped when still a child, and was addicted to heroin, just three of the many burdens that made life difficult for "Lady Day." However, through her recordings she continues to live and share the genius she brought to her music.

BURIED: St. Raymond's Cemetery, Bronx, New York

■

JUDY HOLLIDAY
1921—1965

A bright and beautiful actress, Holliday became a star playing dumb blondes and won an Oscar for her performance in *Born Yesterday*. She died tragically of cancer at the age of forty-four.

BURIED: Westchester Hills Cemetery, Hastings-on-Hudson, New York

■

BUDDY HOLLY
1936—1959

Holly was the leader of The Crickets, and his first hit was "That'll Be the Day" in 1957. Going solo, he released "Peggy Sue," a song that made him a star. While on tour with Ritchie Valens and The Big Bopper, all three were killed in a plane crash. Only twenty-three at the time of his death, his small legacy continues to inspire musicians as diverse as Paul McCartney and Elvis Costello.

BURIED: City of Lubbock Cemetery, Lubbock, Texas

■

WINSLOW HOMER
1836—1910

The New England-born landscape and marine artist began his career as a magazine illustrator, but after becoming financially secure, he devoted himself to painting. Homer spent the last twenty-five years of his life as a complete recluse wintering in Florida and summering in Maine.

BURIED: Mt. Auburn Cemetery, Cambridge, Massachusetts

■

EDWARD HOPPER
1882—1967

An American painter of light and isolation, he lived a simple life with his wife, Jo, in New York City and on Cape Cod. His ability to remain silent was legendary. Considered by many to be one of the greatest painters of the twentieth century, his popularity remains intact even though his work has gradually lost favor with critics.

BURIED: Oak Hill Cemetery, Nyack, New York

■

J. EDGAR HOOVER
1895—1972

As the director of the FBI for almost half a century, from 1924 until his death, he fought both gangsters and communists with a paranoid zeal that bordered on the insane. It was said that Hoover possessed so much dirt on the eight presidents he served that he could not be fired without unleashing the threat of blackmail. He was so powerful that even his alleged homosexuality could not rout him out of office.

BURIED: Congressional Cemetery, Washington, D.C.

■

VLADIMIR HOROWITZ
1904—1989

He played the piano like no one else, winning audiences wherever he went with his virtuosity and personal charm. After fleeing his native Russia, he conquered the concert halls of Europe, moving permanently to America in 1940. He was married to Arturo Toscanini's daughter; with her he made a "farewell" visit to the Soviet Union after glasnost created a welcoming atmosphere. It was one of his final concerts, witnessed by the Russian people as well as millions of television viewers, who were able to watch via a live worldwide satellite linkup.

BURIED: Toscanini Family Plot, Cimitero Monumentale, Milan, Italy

■

HARRY HOUDINI
1874—1926

The magician, who conquered America and was as famous as the president, died on Halloween after having a premonition about his own demise.

BURIED: Machpelah Cemetery, Westchester, New York

JEROME "CURLY" HOWARD
1903—1952

SHEMP HOWARD
1901—1955

These are two of the Three Stooges.

BURIED: Home of Peace Cemetery, Los Angeles, California

ROCK HUDSON
1925—1985

The film star, who epitomized the American male in films like *Pillow Talk* and *Giant*, shocked the world by dying of AIDS. With his good looks, easy smile, and sexual magnetism, he was a major star in Hollywood for decades. Although he never publicly acknowledged either his sexual preference or the nature of his illness, his death drew much-needed attention to the epidemic and galvanized the community into a fundraising frenzy (headed by his friend Elizabeth Taylor). Just before his death a statement reportedly written by Hudson was read to the press by Burt Lancaster. This press release, which brought Rock out of the closet and admitted he was dying of AIDS, itself remains clouded in mystery, since the star was apparently comatose when it was written.

CREMATED: Ashes scattered on the Pacific Ocean

■

LANGSTON HUGHES
1902—1967

As one of the first African-American poets to receive critical attention, he depicted the plight of urban blacks with lyricism, accuracy, and humor. He first published *Shakespeare in Harlem*, a collection of poems, then wrote a relatively successful play called *Mulatto*. After his death, his fame increased and he was immortalized in song by the "Empress of Soul,"

Nina Simone, in her scathing but brilliant "Backlash Blues." Hughes told the story of his own life in a two-volume autobiography: *The Big Sea* and *I Wonder as I Wander*.

CREMATED: Ashes interred beneath the floor of the Hughes Auditorium, Schomburg Center for Research in Black Culture, New York, New York

■

VICTOR HUGO
1802—1885

Considered one of the great French poets of the nineteenth century, he also wrote several successful plays and a novel that has stood the test of time, *Les Miserables*, which has been made into both a film and an international hit musical.

BURIED: The Pantheon, Paris, France

■

JOHN HUSTON
1906—1987

Hollywood director of such classics as *The Maltese Falcon, The African Queen*, and *Moby Dick*, this hard-drinking actor, writer, and filmmaker was adored by the actors he directed, including his father, Walter Huston, and his daughter, Anjelica Huston. Thought to be washed-up in the 1960s after he bombed with *The Bible*, he came back in the 1970s and 1980s, first with *Chinatown* and later with *Prizzi's Honor* (for which his daughter won an Oscar).

BURIED: Hollywood Memorial Park, Los Angeles, California

ALDOUS HUXLEY
1894—1963

The British writer, famous for his novel *Brave New World*, claimed to have cured himself of failing eyesight, a miracle that was vehemently denied by those who knew him well. His critical reputation faded when he moved to California to pursue experiments with mescaline (which resulted in the works *The Doors of Perception* and *Island*), mysticism, and parapsychology.

BURIED: Compton Surrey, England

WASHINGTON IRVING
1783–1859

The man whose name became a household word after publishing his tales "Rip Van Winkle" and "The Legend of Sleepy Hollow" was the first American writer to achieve international fame. While serving as a diplomat to Spain, he produced a biography of Christopher Columbus, and he later published a definitive five-volume biography of George Washington.

BURIED: Sleepy Hollow Cemetery, Tarrytown, New York

■

MAHALIA JACKSON
1911–1972

Raised in a strict, religious household, she never performed in clubs or cabarets, only in recital halls or churches. Nurtured by hymns as well as the singing of Bessie Smith, she was one of the first singers in America to explore the relationship between gospel and rhythm and blues, a musical form labeled pop-gospel by the media. Although she performed most often for white audiences, she sang "Precious Lord" at Martin Luther King, Jr.'s funeral. When she died, over fifty thousand people viewed her coffin, Aretha Franklin performed at the funeral, and there were tributes from all over the world, including several from American presidents.

BURIED: Providence Memorial Park, New Orleans, Louisiana

■

HENRY JAMES
1843—1916

Educated at Harvard and in Europe, James left America to become a British subject, and it was in his adopted England that he wrote the many psychological novels that some find unreadable and others consider classics of the genre. His work was instrumental in creating what was to become known as stream-of-consciousness writing. A confirmed bachelor, he tried and failed to become a playwright before returning to novels, producing such works as *Daisy Miller*, *The Bostonians*, and *The Golden Bowl*.

BURIED: City of Cambridge Cemetery, Cambridge, Massachusetts

■

JESSE JAMES
1847—1882

This cold-blooded killer, who robbed banks and trains, was an American hero. When unarmed, he was shot in the head by a member of his own gang who wanted the reward; the gun had been a gift from Jesse to the killer.

BURIED: Mt. Olive Cemetery, Kearney, Missouri

■

GEORGE JESSEL
1898—1981

As a hoofer in vaudeville, Jessel was lured to Hollywood and offered the starring role in *The Jazz Singer*, a part he turned down. When the film was released, Al Jolson became an overnight sensation and a box office star, a success that eluded Jessel for the rest of his life. After appearing in minor roles in films such as *Stage Door Canteen*, he became a successful producer of musicals like *Wait Till the Sun Shines, Nellie* and wrote the autobiographical *The World I Live In*.

BURIED: Hillside Memorial Park, Los Angeles, California

■

ROBERT JOHNSON
1912—1938

Probably the most influential blues singer, guitarist, and composer of his time, Johnson recorded just twenty-nine songs that helped shape the musical revolution of the 1960s. Poisoned by whiskey laced with strychnine (some say by a jealous girlfriend) at the age of twenty-six, his unique approach to the Mississippi Delta Blues has been preserved for future generations by his record company, which also contributed the funds to preserve and maintain his much-visited gravesite. In addition to his original sessions, his work was recorded by others, including the Rolling Stones ("Love in Vain") and Cream ("Crossroads").

BURIED: Mt. Zion Missionary Baptist Church Cemetery, Morgan City, Mississippi

■

AL JOLSON
1886—1950

An American success story if there ever was one, Al Jolson was a Russian-born American Jew who made it to the top wearing blackface and singing songs like "Mammy" and "Swanee." His first film, *The Jazz Singer*, was the first successful talkie ever made, and it changed both Hollywood and the world to such an

150

extent that the planet's cultural history might be divided into before and after *The Jazz Singer*.

BURIED: Hillside Memorial Park, Los Angeles, California

■

BRIAN JONES
1943—1969

As the guiding hand behind the early Rolling Stones, he helped change the world of music with his contributions to what many consider the best rock-and-roll band ever. Hooked on drugs and with an apparently voracious appetite for sex (a photograph reportedly exists that shows twenty-five women of various ethnic and racial groups with an equal number of children, all claiming to be his), Jones quit the Stones a month before he was found dead, floating in a swimming pool in England. The question of whether he died of an overdose, drowning, or foul play is still unanswered.

BURIED: Cheltenham Cemetery, Cheltenham, Sussex, England

■

JIM JONES
1913—1978

This charismatic cult leader persuaded his Christian followers to commit mass suicide by drinking Kool-Aid and cyanide at their headquarters in Guyana. Of the 917 people who died that day, 248 unclaimed bodies are buried in Evergreen Cemetery, Oakland, California.

CREMATED: Ashes scattered at sea

■

SPIKE JONES
1911—1965

This diminutive bandleader became famous for his clever rearrangements of well-known songs that transformed them into comedy routines; his recording "Der Führer's Face" sold millions in 1942. Jones also appeared in several film musicals including *Thank Your Lucky Stars*.

BURIED: Holy Cross Cemetery, Culver City, California

■

JANIS JOPLIN
1943—1970

When she walked out on stage at the Monterey Pop Festival wearing pink mules with pom-poms and a feather boa, Joplin hushed the crowd to a whisper. When she opened her mouth and her vocal cords belted out the Big Mama Thornton tune "Ball and Chain," jaws dropped (especially Mama Cass's), and the audience witnessed a performance that stood—and remains—the standard for white soul singing in America. First with Big Brother and the Holding Company and later with The Full Tilt Boogie Band, Janis defined rock music in the same way that Billie Holiday defined jazz. Her death of a drug overdose at the age of twenty-seven left a void that has yet to be filled.

CREMATED: Ashes scattered over the Pacific Ocean

■

JAMES JOYCE
1882—1941

Born in Dublin, Ireland, where he published a book of lyrics called *Chamber Music*, he emigrated to Zürich, Switzerland, where he wrote his next two books, *Dubliners* and *Portrait of the Artist as a Young Man*. After moving to Paris in 1920 (where he remained until 1940), he published his masterwork, *Ulysses*, a book that altered the course of world literature forever. Near the end of his life he published his final work,

Finnegans Wake, a novel that again showed his obsession for using words as musical notes and which is incomprehensible to most readers.

BURIED: Fluntern Cemetery, Zürich, Switzerland

■

FRANZ KAFKA
1883—1924

After a lonely and desperate childhood in Prague, where two of his brothers contracted tuberculosis and died young, Kafka turned inward and produced the unforgettable *Metamorphosis*. Raised without tradition in a nonpracticing Jewish household and terrified of the opposite sex, he had a long relationship as a suitor through the mail; he eventually married shortly before dying of the tubercular condition that plagued him most of his life.

BURIED: Jewish Cemetery, Straschnitz, Prague, Czechoslovakia

■

FRIDA KAHLO
1907—1954

At the age of eighteen this great Mexican artist was struck by a bus; the accident left her crippled and unable to have children. She taught herself to paint while lying in bed and spent the rest of her tumultuous life portraying both her physical pain as well as her emotional anguish. Married to an unfaithful Diego Rivera and mistress to both Isamu Noguchi and Leon Trotsky, she painted until the very end of her life, leaving behind a rich and haunting legacy.

CREMATED: Ashes in a jar on top of her bed, Frida Kahlo Museum, Mexico City, Mexico

■

BUSTER KEATON
1895—1956

This great silent film comedian was famous for never smiling. He appeared in such classics as *Limelight*, *Sunset Boulevard*, and *A Funny Thing Happened on the Way to the Forum*.

BURIED: Forest Lawn Hollywood Hills, Los Angeles, California

■

JOHN KEATS
1795–1821

After abandoning the study of medicine, Keats turned to poetry, and his collection *Lamia, Isabella, The Eve of St. Agnes and Other Poems* is widely considered the most important volume of poetry published in England during the nineteenth century. As one of the great Romantic poets (along with Shelley and Byron) his poems "Ode to a Nightingale" and "Ode on a Grecian Urn" remain classics of the genre. His death from tuberculosis at the age of twenty-five added to the mystique of the suffering and tragic young poet.

BURIED: Protestant Cemetery, Rome, Italy

■

HELEN KELLER
1880–1968

The blind American educator's relationship with her teacher, Annie Sullivan, changed the way the nation viewed blindness. A play based on her early years became both a successful Broadway drama and a film entitled *The Miracle Worker*. Hailed as a maverick in the cause of liberating the disabled, she became the confidante of presidents and celebrities and never lost her sense of humor. When asked by a reporter if she closed her eyes when she slept, she replied, "I don't know; I never stayed up long enough to find out."

BURIED: National Cathedral, Washington, D.C.

■

EMMETT KELLY
1898—1979

Unlike most clowns, Kelly's "Weary Willie" had a sad face as he chased elusive spotlights across the stage or the circus floor. Perhaps the most famous clown in America, he performed in The Ringling Brothers, Barnum and Bailey Circus for many years and also entertained the crowd at baseball games.

BURIED: Rest Haven Memorial Park Cemetery, La-fayette, Indiana

■

GRACE KELLY
1929—1982

The American film star, who married the Prince of Monaco in a storybook wedding that enthralled millions, was born in Philadelphia to wealthy parents who were not in the social register (probably because they were Irish). She began her career opposite Gary Cooper in *High Noon*, a film that established her as a major new star. After making two films for Alfred Hitchcock—*Rear Window* and *To Catch a Thief*—she retired from Hollywood and became the princess of Monaco. Mortally injured in an automobile accident, her adoring subjects were told her condition was satisfactory while in fact she was in a coma. Death occurred after the royal family agreed with the doctors that her life-support system be disconnected.

BURIED: Grimaldi Family Vault, Cathedral of St. Nicholas, Monaco

JOHN F. KENNEDY
1917—1963

One of the bestselling 45's of 1961 was the recording of John F. Kennedy's inauguration speech, which included the famous slogan, "Ask not what your country can do for you; ask what you can do for your country." During his brief term as president he was consistently thwarted by Congress and actually accomplished very little while still alive. He did manage, however, to start the Peace Corps and bring the world to the brink of World War III during the Cuban Missile Crisis. He also brought glamour to the White House. With his movie star looks and his beautiful wife by his side, it was said that his administration "would do for sex what the Eisenhowers did for golf." Nicknamed Jack the Zipper, he had several extramarital affairs with Hollywood starlets, and when he grew tired of Marilyn Monroe, he allegedly passed her on to his younger brother, Bobby. It was his death in Texas by an assassin's bullet that gave him a place in the hearts of the American people. The nation was galvanized by the media's coverage of the tragedy, and for a few days America was a nation united in grief.

BURIED: Arlington National Cemetery, Arlington, Virginia

JACK KEROUAC
1922—1969

On the Road, Kerouac's rambling semi-autobiographical novel, is considered a classic; it inspired the generation who came of age in the late 1950s. The most famous writer of the Beat Generation, he became a cult figure more for his life-style than for his work.

BURIED: Edison Cemetery, Lowell, Massachusetts

■

NIKITA KHRUSHCHEV
1894—1971

Born in the Ukraine, this son of a coal miner joined the Communist Party after the revolution of 1917. When Stalin came to power, he put young Nikita in charge of revitalizing Soviet agriculture, and when the murderous dictator died, Khrushchev became First Party Secretary, denounced his former boss, got rid of his rivals in the Politburo, and became premier in 1959. Famous for banging his shoe on his desk at the U.N. and for his on-camera badgering of Richard M. Nixon, the leader who threatened to "bury" the West fell from grace after his perceived bungling of the Cuban Missile Crisis.

BURIED: Novo Devich Cemetery, Moscow, USSR

■

PERCY KILBRIDE
1888—1964

"Pa Kettle" starred with Marjorie Main in the "Ma and Pa Kettle" movies, which portrayed a poor farm family that had enormous warmth and humor.

BURIED: San Bruno/Golden Gate National Cemetery, San Francisco, California

DOROTHY KILGALLEN
1913—1965

The New York journalist's name became a household word as a panelist on television's "What's My Line?" Her face was as easy to recognize as to caricature due to a lack of a chin. Her mysterious death made the headlines as a suicide, although there are those who believe she was murdered because of something she had discovered about the assassination of John F. Kennedy.

BURIED: Gates of Heaven, Mt. Pleasant, New York

MARTIN LUTHER KING, JR.
1929—1968

This great American came to prominence in the 1950s by advocating passive resistance to racial segregation. A moving orator, he led a yearlong boycott of bus companies in Montgomery, Alabama, and then set up the Southern Christian Leadership Conference (SCLC) as a base for his nonviolent civil rights movement. Awarded the Nobel Prize for Peace in 1964, his leadership was challenged by the more militant voices in the African American community. He was murdered in Memphis, Tennessee, while organizing the multiracial Poor People's March for antipoverty legislation. Even though his birthday is now celebrated as a national holiday by most Americans, his dream of a society free of racial discrimination remains just a dream.

BURIED: Southview Cemetery, Atlanta, Georgia

■

ALFRED KINSEY
1894—1956

The American sexologist graduated with a Ph.D. in entomology and became the world's leading authority on the gall wasp before he was hired to teach sex education at Indiana University. He was shocked to find no studies on the subject, so he conducted his own. *The Kinsey Report* was published primarily for the scientific community, but it became a best-seller that helped bring about the sexual revolution of the 1960s.

BURIED: Rose Hill Cemetery, Bloomington, Indiana

■

FRANZ KLINE
1910—1962

Using a photographic enlarger to project images onto his canvas, this abstract expressionist used house paint and quick-drying enamels to create his large black-and-white ideograms.

BURIED: Hollenback Cemetery, Wilkes-Barre, Pennsylvania

■

MARY JO KOPECHNE
1940—1969

The tragic drowning of this young woman in the waters off Chappaquiddick Island when a car driven by Ted Kennedy plunged off a bridge started a media circus on Martha's Vineyard. Was it an accident? What had been her relationship to the senator? Had he been drinking? Could she have been saved? These are all questions that people continue to ask to this day. One thing seems certain; Senator Kennedy's presidential ambitions have been somewhat curtailed by the tragedy.

BURIED: Plymouth, Pennsylvania

∎

ERNIE KOVACS
1914—1962

This pioneer genius of television created characters such as Percy Dovetonsils, J. Walter Puppybreath, Pierre Ragout and Wolfgang Sauerbraten while extending the boundaries of visual humor. His cult following was devastated by his death in a car crash while he was driving home intoxicated from a party at the home of Billy Wilder. He left behind a legacy of truly original humor as well as several million dollars in debts. At the funeral Jack Lemmon placed a cigar in Kovacs' jacket pocket just before he was buried.

BURIED: Forest Lawn, Glendale, California

∎

ALAN LADD
1913—1964

Playing the title character in the Western *Shane*, Alan Ladd found not only the role of his career but also a place in film history. Playing opposite the child star Brandon de Wilde, Ladd had also found a costar he could tower over; in other films he was forced to stand on a wooden box so that the close-up kiss could be planted squarely on the heroine's lips.

BURIED: Forest Lawn, Glendale, California

■

FIORELLO LA GUARDIA
1882—1947

Dubbed the Little Flower, he was mayor of New York City for three consecutive terms and was much loved by his constituents for ridding the city of the political bosses who had ruled by corruption for decades.

BURIED: Woodlawn Cemetery, Bronx, New York

■

BERT LAHR
1895—1967

The rubber-faced comic actor appeared as the Cowardly Lion in *The Wizard of Oz* and on stage in Samuel Beckett's *Waiting for Godot*.

BURIED: Union Field Cemetery, Westchester, New York

■

VERONICA LAKE
1919—1973

Known as the "Peekaboo Girl" because her luxurious blonde hair fell forward over one eye, she was as famous for her tresses as she was for her acting in films like *Sullivan's Travels*, *This Gun for Hire*, and *I Married a Witch*. When she cut her hair, her career came to a screeching halt, and she ended up waiting on tables at a restaurant in New York City.

CREMATED: Ashes scattered in the Caribbean

■

ELSA LANCHESTER
1902—1986

The bride of Frankenstein in films and the wife of
Charles Laughton in reality, her career flourished for
decades. Her unforgettable hair style as the monster's
bride, which thrust upward like the Leaning Tower of
Pisa, may have been the model for the animated cartoon character Marge Simpson.

CREMATED: Ashes scattered at sea

■

MARIO LANZA
1921—1959

This Italian-American tenor conquered America with
his mellifluous voice and his rugged good looks in the
film biography *The Great Caruso*. Prone to excessive
eating and drinking, he was deemed too fat to appear
in the film version of *The Student Prince*, but his voice
supplied the notes coming out of actor Edmund Pur-
dom's mouth.

BURIED: Holy Cross Cemetery, Culver City, California

■

CHARLES LAUGHTON
1899—1962

Whether he was strolling the decks in *Mutiny on the Bounty*, wheeling through the courtroom in *Witness for the Prosecution*, or swinging through the rafters as *The Hunchback of Notre Dame*, this decidedly homely actor commanded the viewer's complete attention. Scorned by some—including Alfred Hitchcock—for his apparent homosexuality, he nevertheless prevailed as a star with the complete cooperation of his wife, Elsa Lanchester.

BURIED: Forest Lawn Hollywood Hills, Los Angeles, California

■

STAN LAUREL
1890—1965

Originally an understudy for Charlie Chaplin, he went on to have a promising solo career. When he teamed up with Oliver Hardy, the duo became American icons. *The Music Box*, starring Laurel and Hardy, won an Oscar as Best Short of the Year, but Hollywood soon forgot about Stan Laurel, and he died penniless and alone in a Los Angeles rooming house.

BURIED: Forest Lawn, Glendale, California

■

D. H. LAWRENCE
1885—1930

The English poet and novelist, who was discovered by
Ford Madox Ford, was suspected of being a German
spy during World War I (his wife was German) and of
being a fascist during World War II. He espoused a
philosophy that centered around the necessity of man's
union with nature and the need for a superhuman
leader. His most famous novels are *Sons and Lovers*,
Women in Love, and the infamous *Lady Chatterley's
Lover*, a book banned in England and America for
many years.

CREMATED: Ashes interred in the altar, The Chapel of
Kiowa Ranch, Taos, New Mexico

■

GERTRUDE LAWRENCE
1898—1952

A childhood friend of Noël Coward, this English actress and singer appeared with him in his play *Private
Lives*. Later successes included the musicals *Lady in
the Dark* and *The King and I* (written for her by Rodg-
ers and Hammerstein) and a film version of Tennessee
Williams's *The Glass Menagerie*. She is buried wearing
the pink satin ball gown she wore in *The King and I*
when she sang the classic "Shall We Dance?"

BURIED: The Aldrich Plot, Parkview Cemetery, Up-
ton, Massachusetts

■

BRUCE LEE
1940—1973

Born in San Francisco but raised in Hong Kong, Bruce began studying martial arts at the age of thirteen. After returning to the United States and graduating from the University of Washington, he founded Kung-Fu academies along the West Coast and became an actor on television. Back in Hong Kong he starred in a series of low-budget, high-profit films including *Fists of Fury*, *The Chinese Dragon* and his last, *Enter the Dragon*. His death remains a mystery.

BURIED: Lakeview Cemetery, Seattle, Washington

■

ROBERT E. LEE
1807—1870

The supreme commander of the Confederate Army during the Civil War was a graduate of West Point and the husband of George and Martha Washington's great-granddaughter. His loyalty to the South took precedence over his distaste for secession and slavery, and he kept the Confederacy hopeful until his defeat at Gettysburg. After regrouping his troops, he tried again but was ultimately defeated by Ulysses S. Grant at Appomattox, which brought the war to an end.

BURIED: Lee Chapel Museum, Washington and Lee University, Lexington, Virginia

■

VIVIEN LEIGH
1913—1967

Although she was as English as the Queen Mother, she was chosen to play the most famous southern belle of all time, Scarlett O'Hara, in *Gone with the Wind*, for which she won her first Academy Award. Married for a time to Laurence Olivier, she won her second Oscar as Blanche Du Bois, Tennessee Williams's fading femme fatale in *A Streetcar Named Desire*. Slipping in and out of mental health during the last years of her life, she toured in the musical *Tovarich* before succumbing to illness at her home outside London.

CREMATED: Ashes scattered on the lake at her country estate, Tickerage Hill, near London, England

■

VLADIMIR LENIN
1870—1924

The Bolshevik Revolution of 1917 could not have succeeded without this Russian political hero. A staunch Marxist, he allied himself with both Trotsky and Stalin, adopting the name Lenin in order to avoid persecution in his career as a revolutionary.

BURIED: Body on display, Red Square, Moscow, USSR

■

JOHN LENNON
1940—1980

Widely considered the most intelligent and political member of the Beatles, Lennon's collaboration with Paul McCartney produced some of the most beautiful, successful, and influential music of the twentieth century. After the breakup of the Fab Four and the bitter estrangement from McCartney, Lennon wrote the song "Imagine," a tune that has become an anthem and a word that graces Strawberry Fields, his memorial in New York's Central Park. Murdered by a deranged fan outside the Dakota, the apartment building where he lived with his wife, Yoko Ono, and son, Sean, his death shocked millions and signaled the end of an era.

CREMATED: Some ashes scattered in England and some cast in the wind in Strawberry Fields, Central Park, New York, New York

■

LOTTE LENYA
1900—1981

Born in Vienna, Lenya (as everyone who knew her called her) began her career on the stage doing Shakespeare, but after marrying the composer Kurt Weill, she found her true calling in Berlin by starring in the musicals her husband wrote with Bertolt Brecht. Beginning with *The Little Mahagonny* (the first collaboration), she then took on the role of Jenny in *The Threepenny Opera* and became an international star during its five-year run. Escaping Nazi Germany in 1933, she and Weill moved first to Paris and then to the United States, where they remained for the rest of their lives. In a mid-1950s revival of the *Opera*, she won a Tony Award as Jenny (singing in English). Her unmistakable and unforgettable gravelly voice is preserved on the recordings she made, and her films include Tennessee Williams's *The Roman Spring of Mrs. Stone* and one of Ian Fleming's James Bond megahits, *From Russia with Love*.

BURIED: Mt. Repose Cemetery, Haverstraw, New York

■

LEONARDO DA VINCI
1452—1519

As a writer, scientist, architect, and painter, Leonardo embodied the ideals of the Renaissance man. During his first years in Florence, he painted *The Adoration of the Magi*, then in Milan he created the famous fresco *The Last Supper*. For most of his adult life he traveled back and forth between these two cities, studying anatomy, painting, and practicing architecture. In his later years he worked at the Vatican, although Michelangelo and Raphael were already ensconced as artists-in-residence. Leaving town with the Pope's brother, Giuliano de' Medici, he spent his final days in France, where he finally died.

BURIED: Originally interred at Amboise, France; his remains were later cremated and scattered during the Wars of Religion

■

OSCAR LEVANT
1906—1972

Pianist, composer, wit, actor, writer, and intellectual, he claimed in his autobiography, *Memoirs of an Amnesiac*, to have erased the fine line between genius and insanity. Levant became famous on radio, on television, and in movies like *An American in Paris* as a depressed pianist with an acerbic tongue. Addicted to drugs for most of his life, he tried with some success to escape the pain he perceived as reality.

BURIED: Westwood Memorial Park, Los Angeles, California

SINCLAIR LEWIS
1885—1951

After turning down a Pulitzer Prize, this novelist became the first American writer to receive the Nobel Prize. By naming one of his characters Babbitt and describing him perceptively, he unintentionally added a new word to the English language.

BURIED: Protestant Cemetery, Rome, Italy

LIBERACE
1919—1987

Famous for his outrageous clothes and jewelry as well as his skill at the piano, he seemed an unlikely candidate for television stardom, especially in the bland, repressive 1950s. But America's growing TV audience loved him; his career spanned several decades and revolutions in taste, both musical and moral. At the end of his life he was a bigger success than ever, and although he denied having AIDS, an autopsy proved otherwise. The Liberace Museum charges six dollars a head and its attendance record rivals Graceland's.

BURIED: Forest Lawn Hollywood Hills, Los Angeles, California

ABRAHAM LINCOLN
1809—1865

Six-feet four-inches tall, "Honest Abe" was the tallest of the presidents. He was probably not the only one to see ghosts, however, but was the only one to hold seances in the White House in order to talk to his dead children. He also had premonitions of his own assassination while he guided the country through the Civil War. He remains one of America's most admired presidents.

BURIED: Lincoln Tomb, Oakridge Cemetery, Springfield, Illinois

MARY TODD LINCOLN
1818—1882

Rumored to be a Southern spy since most of her family fought the Civil War on the Confederate side, she was intensely disliked by almost everyone. She was the Civil War's Imelda Marcos, spending a fortune on clothes (including hundreds of pairs of gloves), which she stored in boxes hidden in closets. After losing three sons and a husband, and running up a debt of twenty-seven thousand dollars, she accused her last remaining son of stealing all her jewels and was finally committed to a sanitorium.

BURIED: Lincoln Tomb, Oakridge Cemetery, Springfield, Illinois

CHARLES LINDBERGH
1902—1974

The aviator who made the first solo flight across the Atlantic in his plane *The Spirit of St. Louis* (which was also the title of the book that won him a Pulitzer Prize) was treated as an international superstar. He and his wife, Anne Morrow, left the United States and moved to England after their infant son was kidnapped and killed. At the start of World War II he returned to the United States to make antiwar speeches and was branded pro-Nazi, but when America finally entered the fray, he served in the Pacific as a pilot.

BURIED: Kipanula Hawaiian Churchyard, Maui, Hawaii

■

DIANE LINKLETTER
1948—1969

Kids do the darndest things! Daughter of TV personality Art Linkletter, Diane jumped out of the window of her apartment when she was high on LSD and was killed. As a result, she became the object of a cult following, especially after filmmaker John Waters made a movie about her life.

BURIED: Forest Lawn Hollywood Hills, Los Angeles, California

■

CAROLE LOMBARD
1908—1942

She was the wife of Clark Gable and was the "screwball" comedienne just as funny offscreen as she was in her films. Endowed with the kind of beauty that some

compared to Garbo's, she lit up the screen in films like *My Man Godfrey* and (her last) *To Be or Not to Be*, opposite the great Jack Benny. While traveling across the country on a war bond tour (she raised millions for the war effort), she was killed in a plane crash along with her agent and her mother. When Gable died eighteen years later, the press asked his widow where he would be buried. "With Carole, of course. She was his greatest love" was her courageous reply.

BURIED: Forest Lawn, Glendale, California

∎

JACK LONDON
1876—1916

The author of *The Call of the Wild*, the son of an astrologer/spiritualist, London grew up in terrible poverty. A man of many contradictions (he was a Socialist who championed the plight of the common man while holding simultaneously the beliefs of a white supremacist), he slowly destroyed himself with drugs and alcohol.

BURIED: Jack London Park and Museum, Glen Ellen, California

∎

HENRY WADSWORTH LONGFELLOW
1807—1882

Both a poet and a teacher (at Bowdoin and Harvard), he wrote some of the most popular poems in American history; poems that generations of children have had to memorize in school. Among his most memorable works are "Hiawatha," "Paul Revere's Ride," and "The Village Blacksmith." Longfellow was the first American whose bust was placed in Poet's Corner in Westminster Abbey, London, England.

BURIED: Mt. Auburn Cemetery, Cambridge, Massachusetts

PETER LORRE
1904—1964

Although he often played German spies, Lorre was actually born in Hungary and became a star in Hollywood for both his acting ability and his mysterious physical presence. Short, bug-eyed and speaking with an unmistakable but unidentifiable accent, he added another dimension to films like *The Maltese Falcon*, *Casablanca*, and *20,000 Leagues Under the Sea*.

BURIED: Hollywood Memorial Park Cemetery, Los Angeles, California

JOE LOUIS
1914—1981

Nicknamed "The Brown Bomber" by the white press, Louis was the most famous African American in the United States during the 1940s. His first-round knockout in 1938 of Max Schmeling, the German boxer who symbolized Nazism, made Joe Louis the first black American hero to both whites and blacks.

BURIED: Arlington National Cemetery, Arlington, Virginia

■

BELA LUGOSI
1882—1956

The Hungarian actor who played *Dracula* was condemned to suck blood for most of his career. He died a morphine addict and was buried in the caped costume he wore as the Transylvanian Count.

BURIED: Holy Cross Cemetery, Culver City, California

■

ALFRED LUNT
1893—1977
LYNN FONTANNE
1887—1983

The best-loved couple of the American theater appeared in over twenty-seven productions together. Among their many triumphs were *The Visit*, *Design for Living*, and *Pygmalion*. A Broadway theater is named in their honor.

BURIED: Forest Home Cemetery, Milwaukee, Wisconsin

■

CHARLES LUDLAM
1943—1987

Star, founder, and resident genius of the Ridiculous Theatrical Company in New York City, he garnered raves in the *The New York Times* that were usually reserved for visiting British thespians like Olivier and Burton. His most famous role was that of Camille, Dumas's ill-fated heroine portrayed on the screen by Garbo; Ludlam made the play into a tear-jerking farce. Other creations included a temperamental but touching Maria Callas in his tour-de-force *Galas* and a wayward princess in *Salambo*, who tells her faithful female servant (played by Everett Quinton, Ludlam's "longtime companion" and the new director of the company), "Come, shave the delta of my venus." Summoned to Hollywood to play a southern lawyer in *The Big Easy*, his budding film career came to an end when he died of AIDS at forty-four.

BURIED: St. Patrick's Cemetery, Huntington, New York

■

"MOMS" MABLEY
1894—1975

One of the most beloved of entertainers, she entered show business as a child singing in vaudeville and became a star in the 1950s as a stand-up comedienne. With her toothless grin and bag-lady appearance, she crossed the color line and became a familiar guest on the "Jack Paar Show." She also had a hit record in the sixties, "Abraham, Martin, and John," a song about the three assassinated leaders.

BURIED: Ferncliff Cemetery, Hartsdale, New York

■

MAN O' WAR

This racehorse set five world racing records, and when he died, his owners had him embalmed, gave him a formal funeral, and buried him in a satin-lined casket.

BURIED: Kentucky Horse Park, Lexington, Kentucky

■

JAYNE MANSFIELD
1933—1967

This sex symbol of the late 1950s, whose on-screen performances were memorable not for her minimal acting ability but for her maximum cleavage, was decapitated in an automobile accident near Biloxi, Mississippi. The star of such dogs as *Dog Eat Dog*, *Hercules in the Vale of Woe* and *The Girl Can't Help It* (for which Little Richard sang the title song) drove a pink Cadillac convertible, which is on display at the Tragedy in U.S. History Museum in St. Augustine, Florida.

BURIED: Fairview Cemetery, Pen Argyl, Pennsylvania

■

ROCKY MARCIANO
1924—1969

One year after becoming one of only two boxers who defeated the great Joe Louis by knockout, he became the Heavyweight Champion of the World, a title he did not relinquish until he retired undefeated in 1956. This much-loved American champion died in a plane crash at the age of forty-five.

BURIED: Lauderdale Memorial Gardens, Fort Lauderdale, Florida

BOB MARLEY
1945—1981

With his band The Wailers, Marley became a star as well as a hero in his native Jamaica. Like many of his countrymen he was a Rastafarian, and he put the words of their religious leader, Haile Selassie, to music that became known around the world as "reggae." Less successful in America at first, he hit the charts with "No Woman No Cry" and wrote the immensely successful *I Shot the Sheriff*, recorded by Eric Clapton. During a visit to New York City he had a stroke while jogging in Central Park and died not long after of cancer in Miami, Florida.

BURIED: Rhoden Hall, St. Ann's Parish, Jamaica

CHICO MARX
1886—1961

As the brother of Groucho and Harpo, he appeared in all the Marx Brothers' films. In his private life he was a compulsive gambler.

BURIED: Forest Lawn, Glendale, California

■

GROUCHO MARX
1890—1977

One of America's most famous comedians, who along with his brothers Chico and Harpo appeared in vaudeville as the Marx Brothers, he became an American cultural treasure in films like *Duck Soup*, *A Night at the Opera*, and *A Day at the Races*. Working alone, Groucho was the host of "You Bet Your Life," a TV game show that kept Americans laughing for years.

BURIED: Eden Memorial Park, Los Angeles, California

■

KARL MARX
1818—1883

The German-born Father of Communism, Marx moved to Paris and allied himself with Friedrich Engels, with whom he wrote *The Communist Manifesto*, an exposition of the working-class struggle. One of the great intellectuals of his or any other age, he was feared and scorned for his revolutionary thinking. After he moved to London, where he spent the rest of his life in poverty, he published *Das Kapital*, the bible of what came to be known as Marxism. Like Christianity, Marxism has never been practiced as its founder intended.

BURIED: Highgate Cemetery, London, England

■

RAYMOND MASSEY
1896—1983

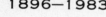

Born into a fine Canadian family (his brother was the governor-general), Massey created two distinct personas in film, the kindly understanding gentleman, and the evil, threatening maniac. Perfect as *Abe Lincoln in Illinois*, he also appeared as the psychotic murderer in *Arsenic and Old Lace*. In the mid-1960s he starred on television as Dr. Gillespie on "Dr. Kildare."

BURIED: Beaverdale Memorial Cemetery, New Caanan, Connecticut

■

COTTON MATHER
1663—1728

As one of the most influential writers and thinkers in the early development of America, this Puritan minister helped establish intolerance as a way of American life. Powerful both in the church and the government in his state of Massachusetts, he roused the God-fearing populace during the Salem witch hunts, using Christianity as an excuse to burn those who were allegedly possessed by the Devil. His moral teachings are still popular among certain fundamentalist religious sects.

BURIED: Copps Hill Burial Ground, Boston, Massachusetts

■

HENRI MATISSE
1869—1954

Perhaps the greatest painter of the modern era, this French artist, along with Picasso, redefined the art of the twentieth century. Confined to bed in his later life and unable to paint, he extended his oeuvre by creating extraordinary paper cutouts of great beauty and clarity. His private life stands as the antithesis to that of the "suffering artist."

BURIED: The Cemetery in Cimiez, France

■

LOUIS B. MAYER
1885—1957

This Russian-born impresario began his career by buy-ing movie theaters in New England and then merging with Sam Goldwyn to form Metro Goldwyn Mayer, one of the most successful film production studios in the history of Hollywood. A power-hungry tycoon, he was known for his domineering, paternalistic stance with the stars he had under contract, ruining careers as well as nurturing them.

BURIED: Home of Peace Cemetery, Los Angeles, California

■

CHARLIE McCARTHY

It should come as no surprise to any observer of Amer-ican pop culture that one of the most successful names in show business history belongs to a wooden dummy. His mouthpiece was Edgar Bergen, father of Candice.

NOT BURIED: On display, Smithsonian Institution, Washington, D.C.

■

JOSEPH McCARTHY
1908—1957

When the junior Senator from Wisconsin appeared on national television in 1954, he ushered in more than the Army-McCarthy hearings; his relentless shouts of "point of order!" became the slogan for an historic smear campaign which ruined the lives and careers of countless innocent people. An obscure lawyer and publicity hound, McCarthy fabricated his own military history and set himself up as a watchdog able to ferret out "commies" in both the government and in Hollywood. In one of the most shameful periods of U.S. history, this closeted homosexual allied himself with Joseph Kennedy (who gave him money) and Francis Cardinal Spellman (who delivered church support). McCarthy's reign of terror finally ended when he was attacked by Edward R. Murrow, fittingly enough, on television.

BURIED: Cemetery of St. Mary's Roman Catholic Church, Appleton, Wisconsin

■

HATTIE McDANIEL
1895—1952

Always a maid but never less than brilliant, she turned her role in *Gone with the Wind* into an Oscar-winning performance. The first black American to win the coveted prize, her articulate and gracious acceptance

speech belied Hollywood's tawdry habit of casting this great actress in demeaning roles. Her Academy Award did little to change the practice, and she died broken-hearted, never getting another chance to show her great talent.

BURIED: Rosedale Cemetery, Los Angeles, California

■

JEANETTE MacDONALD
1906–1965

The beautiful redhead, who caused opera critics to recoil in horror, filled the movie theaters of America with enough vocal expertise to become one of the most famous stars—and one of the biggest box-office bonanzas—of her time. Teamed with Nelson Eddy in a series of operettas such as *Naughty Marietta* and *Rose Marie*, the pair became the uncrowned "King and Queen of America." They were linked romantically in the press, but the story was always denied by the couple; after their deaths it was revealed that they had been involved in a clandestine affair after all.

BURIED: Forest Lawn, Glendale, California

■

FIBBER McGEE & MOLLY
JAMES JORDAN
1896—1988

MARIAN JORDAN
1898—1961

They were radio's beloved couple who had the famous overcrowded closet. Sound effects people had a field day every time Fibber opened the closet door and years of neglect came tumbling out, making hilarious noises that fired up listeners' imaginations. Their small-town values did not translate into real life however; Molly was an alcoholic and their life together was far from serene.

BURIED: Holy Cross Cemetery, Culver City, California

STEVE McQUEEN
1930—1980

Known for his ability to light up the screen with his tough-but-tender sex appeal in films like *Love with the Proper Stranger*, he could also go it alone, as he did in *Bullitt*, a movie that featured the best car chase ever filmed. From the cult classic *The Blob*, his first starring film, to the *Cincinnati Kid*, McQueen managed to balance that rare combination of masculinity and vulnerability. He also had a successful television series called "Wanted: Dead or Alive" before dying of cancer.

CREMATED: Ashes scattered in Santa Paula Valley, California

■

MARGARET MEAD
1901—1978

As the most famous American anthropologist of her time, Mead's ability to make her studies understandable to the general public was her most important claim to fame. Starting her career as a curator at the American Museum of Natural History in New York City, she did her field work in Samoa and New Guinea on child rearing and later published *The Coming of Age in Samoa, Male and Female,* and *Growth and Culture.*

BURIED: The cemetery in Buckingham, Pennsylvania

■

HERMAN MELVILLE
1819—1891

The self-taught author of *Moby Dick* died virtually a forgotten man; his great novel about the white whale was reviled by contemporary critics and readers, and he was forced to support himself as a clerk in the customs house. His other masterpiece, *Billy Budd*, was published posthumously.

BURIED: Woodlawn Cemetery, Bronx, New York

■

ADOLPH MENJOU
1890—1963

This film star was a right-wing collaborator of Senator Joe McCarthy during the years of the Hollywood witch hunts. Never a leading man, he aptly played the city slicker with a heavy dose of sleaze in such films as *Morning Glory* (with a young Katharine Hepburn) and *A Star Is Born* (with Janet Gaynor). In an effort to bolster his fading film career in Hollywood, Menjou sang like a bird to the House Un-American Activities Committee, betraying friends and coworkers.

BURIED: Hollywood Memorial Park Cemetery, Culver City, California

■

THOMAS MERTON
1915—1968

The religious writer and poet converted to Roman Catholicism while in college, becoming a Trappist monk and priest. He wrote an autobiography called *The Seven Storey Mountain* that began a revival in monastic enrollment, and his many books on Eastern mysticism and Christian meditation sold millions. It was rumored he was about to announce his departure from the Roman Catholic Church, when, on a visit to Thailand for an interdenominational conference, he was accidentally electrocuted in his bath.

BURIED: Monastery at Gethsemane, Nelson County, Kentucky

GRACE METALIOUS
1924—1964

The author of *Peyton Place*, the best-selling book that shocked America, was persona non grata in her own hometown. When she died, she was buried amidst the people who had scorned her despite her express wish that she not be returned to the town that was used as the model for her novel.

BURIED: Smith Meeting House Cemetery, Gilmanton, New Hampshire

HARVEY MILK
1930—1979

The first openly homosexual candidate elected to a government position, Milk was gunned down in his office at San Francisco's City Hall, where he was serving as city supervisor, by ex-fireman, ex-policeman, and ex-supervisor Dan White. His death stunned not only San Francisco and the people who had voted him into office but also the entire nation.

BURIED: Ashes scattered in San Francisco Bay

∎

HENRY MILLER
1891—1980

Sex was the theme for this American writer, who lived and worked in Paris, where he published *Tropic of Cancer* and *Tropic of Capricorn*, both banned in America until the early 1960s. Moving back to the United States, he settled in Big Sur, California, and became a cult figure of the sexual revolution of the 1960s, continuing to produce sexually explicit novels that seemed like erotic postcards from the past.

CREMATED: Ashes scattered in Big Sur, California

∎

SAL MINEO
1939—1976

Made famous by his performance opposite James Dean in *Rebel Without a Cause*, Sal Mineo was murdered in his Hollywood home by a male hustler (according to most reports), but his death is still classified as an unsolved mystery.

BURIED: Gate of Heaven Cemetery, Mt. Pleasant, New York

■

CHARLES MINGUS
1942—1979

Before the age of seventeen he played the cello in the Los Angeles Junior Philharmonic Orchestra, but he then took up the double bass and played with Louis Armstrong, Lionel Hampton, and Duke Ellington. Joining Max Roach, he established a recording company called Debut, one of the first musician-owned studios in America. Considered one of the greatest innovators in jazz, he had no difficulty reconciling writing and improvising and sometimes shouted out instructions during performances. In the 1960s he experimented with a twenty-two-piece band in compositions like "Black Saint and the Sinner Lady" and published an autobiography called *Beneath the Underdog*.

CREMATED: Ashes scattered in the Ganges River, Benares, India

■

CARMEN MIRANDA
1913—1955

The "Brazilian Bombshell" made up for her smallness by wearing hats that looked like the towering fruit centerpieces seen on buffet tables aboard ocean liners. Singing and dancing her way through a series of Hollywood musicals like *Down Argentine Way* and *That Night in Rio*, her American film career came to an abrupt halt when it was discovered that under her swirling skirts she never wore underwear. Her boundless energy was allegedly due to the large amounts of cocaine she smuggled into the country concealed in the very high heels of her platform shoes.

BURIED: Sao Joaobad Trista Cemetery, Rio de Janeiro, Brazil

■

MARGARET MITCHELL
1900—1949

Daughter of the president of the Atlanta Historical Society, it took Mitchell ten years to write her only novel, *Gone with the Wind*, which won a Pulitzer Prize, sold over one million copies in its first year in print, and went on to become the all-time best-seller in U.S. publishing history. It was also a film.

BURIED: Oakland Cemetery, Atlanta, Georgia

■

MARTHA MITCHELL
1918—1976

Known as either The Mouth that Roared or The Watergate Warbler, she was the outspoken wife of Attorney General John Mitchell. Were it not for Martha and her big mouth, the public might never have discovered just how corrupt the Nixon administration really was.

BURIED: Bellwood Cemetery, Pine Bluff, Arkansas

■

TOM MIX
1880—1940

After serving as a soldier in the Spanish-American War, Mix became a box-office star in the 1920s as the quintessential cowboy in four hundred movies like *Riders of the Purple Sage*. Never very comfortable in Hollywood, Mix left Tinseltown to join the circus but returned for financial reasons and made the classic film *Destry Rides Again*. He died in a car crash.

BURIED: Forest Lawn, Glendale, California

■

JEAN BAPTISTE MOLIÈRE
1622—1673

This French actor and playwright exposed the upper classes in his sophisticated comedies and toured the country with a troupe that eventually became the Comédie Française. As writer, director, producer, and star, he staged dozens of farces under the auspices of Louis XIV and died on stage while performing the title role in *The Hypochondriac*. His other successes include *The Misanthrope* and *Tartuffe*.

BURIED: Père Lachaise Cemetery, Paris, France

THELONIOUS MONK
1917—1982

Self-taught as a child, he later studied the piano, and in the 1940s played in Harlem with Dizzy Gillespie, Charlie Parker, and Bud Powell. Together they invented Bebop, one of the most important jazz movements of the fifties.

BURIED: Ferncliff Cemetery, Hartsdale, New York

MARILYN MONROE
1926—1962

As the biggest star Hollywood ever produced, her
name has become part of the American consciousness.
Abused and abandoned as a child, she never fully recovered, and she spent her brief life searching for love.
Her death at the age of thirty-six is clouded in mystery, with both suicide and murder distinct possibili-
ties. The men in her life were equally famous: Joe
DiMaggio, Arthur Miller, and Robert and John F.
Kennedy. Known at first for dumb-blonde roles, Marilyn surprised fans and critics alike with her performances in *Bus Stop* and *The Prince and the Showgirl*,
two of her most memorable films.

BURIED: Westwood Memorial Park, Los Angeles,
California

ALBERTO MORAVIA
1907—1990

This Jewish-Italian author, whose love affair with
Rome lasted a lifetime, was the best-selling modern
writer in Italian literature. Loved and admired by his
countrymen, most of whom lived by the dictates of the
Vatican, he often said that he never gave the existence
of God a thought and remained uninterested in religion
until his death. His work was both political and sexual;
it was banned by both the fascists and the Roman

Catholic Church. Famous for saying that sex was possible without love but love not possible without sex, his books include *The Conformist* and *Two Women*, both of which have been made into modern film classics.

BURIED: Verano Cemetery, Rome, Italy

■

MORRIS THE CAT

The most famous cat in America became a star selling cat food on television. An orange tabby, he epitomized the finicky eater with snob appeal.

BURIED: At the home of his trainer, Chicago, Illinois

■

JIM MORRISON
1943—1971

Lead singer and composer for the rock group The Doors, he personified the emerging archetype of the rock poet. Repeatedly arrested for allegedly exposing himself on stage to fans and for performing fellatio on Jimi Hendrix, he was rebellious, beautiful, intelligent,

sensual, and hooked on drugs. His fame has been elevated to the status of myth ever since his mysterious
death at the age of twenty-seven in a Paris bathtub.
"Light My Fire," The Doors' biggest hit, is often cited
as the most popular song of the sixties, eclipsing all
compositions by the Beatles.

BURIED: Père Lachaise Cemetery, Paris, France

■

GRANDMA MOSES
1860—1961

After living on farms in Virginia and New York for
most of her life, she gave up embroidering country
scenes in wool because of the onset of arthritis, and
at the age of seventy-six she took up painting. She
turned out hundreds of primitive paintings, which sold
like the proverbial hotcakes, and she continued to paint
until after her hundredth birthday.

BURIED: Maple Grove Cemetery, Hoosick Falls, New
York

■

ELIJAH MUHAMMAD
1897—1975

He was the founder and leader of the Black Muslims, The Nation of Islam, and the man who inspired Malcolm X before the two separated due to irreconcilable differences.

BURIED: Mount Glenwood Cemetery, Glenwood, Illinois

■

AUDIE MURPHY
1924—1971

After becoming the most decorated soldier of World War II, he made over forty films in Hollywood and had the starring role in his own film biography, *To Hell and Back*.

BURIED: Arlington National Cemetery, Arlington, Virginia

■

VLADIMIR NABOKOV
1899—1977

It's not surprising that the Russian author of *Lolita* had a pathological dread of Jane Austen. Nabokov's reputation as one of the most original prose writers of the twentieth century comes in part from his relentlessly masculine viewpoint and somewhat scatological subject matter. He was born in St. Petersburg, studied in Cambridge, then lived in Paris and Berlin. In 1940 he moved to the United States and taught at Wellesley, Stanford, Cornell, and Harvard, living an academic-bohemian life. In 1961 he moved to Switzerland for tax purposes.

BURIED: Clarens Cemetery, Clarens, Switzerland

■

CARRY NATION
1846—1911

Hatchet in hand, Carry Nation would walk into saloons and destroy every bottle of booze in sight. She believed she was appointed by God to rid mankind of "Demon Rum." Arrested and thrown in jail over thirty times, her fiery oratory actually helped pass the Eighteenth Amendment of the Constitution, which ushered in Prohibition.

BURIED: Belton Cemetery, Belton, Missouri

■

ALLA NAZIMOVA
1879—1945

Famous for her performances of Ibsen's heroines on the European stage, this Russian actress came to Hollywood and became a silent film star. Allegedly homosexual, she became a lesbian cult figure and was rumored to be the lover of Valentino's wife, Natasha Rambova. She caused an enormous scandal by leaking a story to the press that the entire cast of *Salome* was gay. In her later years she appeared as Tyrone Power's mother in *Blood and Sand*.

BURIED: Forest Lawn, Glendale, California

OZZIE NELSON
1906—1975

His resemblance to singing star Rudy Vallee was so pronounced that young Ozzie bought a megaphone and started a band. He married Harriet Hilliard and was given a radio program, *The Adventures of Ozzie and Harriet*, that lasted for twenty-two years, first on radio and then on television.

BURIED: Forest Lawn Hollywood Hills, Los Angeles, California

VASLAV NIJINSKY
1890—1950

Considered to have been the greatest male dancer of all time, Nijinsky's life was filled with tragedy. It was discovered early in Vaslav's life that he had only one ability: he could dance. When he graduated from the Russian Imperial School of Ballet, he came under the influence of the impresario Diaghilev, who became his lover and mentor, encouraging the young dancer to choreograph his own ballets. At the pinnacle of his career, schizophrenia surfaced, and he abandoned Diaghilev to marry Romola de Polsky. Diaghilev, who was furious, fired him, severing Nijinsky from the ballet company. Soon after, he fell into a decline and never danced again.

BURIED: Montmartre Cemetery, Paris, France

ANAÏS NIN
1903—1977

So obsessed with herself that she published six volumes of her diaries, thereby creating a new genre of feminist literature, Anaïs Nin also wrote erotica, novels, criticism, and essays. Her ménage à trois with Henry Miller and his wife June was made into a film.

BURIED: Swan Point Cemetery, Providence, Rhode Island

RAMON NOVARRO
1899—1968

Second only to Rudolph Valentino in popularity, this Latin lover was the star of the 1925 *Ben-Hur*. His career ended in 1935 when studio heads determined that his homosexuality was too great a risk. He tried directing and singing, and he eventually wound up on television in *Bonanza*. At the age of sixty-nine he was beaten to death by two male hustlers. One thousand people attended his funeral, and the day after he was buried, the two killers were caught; they were tried and sentenced to life imprisonment.

BURIED: Calvary Cemetery, Los Angeles, California

ANNIE OAKLEY
1860—1926

The most famous female gunslinger of all time toured for fifteen years with Buffalo Bill's Wild West Show.

BURIED: Brock Cemetery, Greenville, Ohio

CLIFFORD ODETS
1906—1963

Playwright Odets helped form the Group Theater with Lee Strasberg, Elia Kazan, Harold Clurman, and Stella Adler. His first produced play, *Waiting for Lefty*, was an overnight success, and his career flourished on both coasts. He was married for a time to the actress Louise Rainer.

BURIED: Forest Lawn, Glendale, California

■

FRANK O'HARA
1926—1966

Run over by a beach taxi on Fire Island, Frank O'Hara left behind a largely unpublished body of work. Well-known as a curator at the Museum of Modern Art in New York and celebrated by the Whitney Museum with an exhibition called A Poet Among Painters, he single-handedly determined the direction of American painting in the 1960s simply by purchasing the works of his friends. His fame and influence as a poet was posthumous but profound.

BURIED: Green River Cemetery, East Hampton, New York

■

JOHN O'HARA
1905–1970

Among the finest short-story writers in English, he published more stories (a total of 225) in *The New Yorker* than any other writer. The son of a doctor, he never graduated from college, was terribly defensive (he called critics "little old ladies of both sexes"), and a great snob. On his gravestone are these words, which he wrote himself: "Better than anyone else, he told the truth about his time . . ." His ego was monumental, and he suffered great paranoia, severing decades-old friendships over imagined slights. He won a National Book Award for *Ten North Frederick*, and his novel *Pal Joey* was made into a film and a Broadway musical.

BURIED: Princeton Cemetery, Princeton, New Jersey

■

WARNER OLAND
1880–1938

Born in Sweden, he came to Hollywood to play Dr. Fu Manchu and later created the role of Charlie Chan, which he played in more than a dozen films. With his ingenious use of makeup, his audience never knew that he was not Chinese.

BURIED: Rural Cemetery, Southborough, Massachusetts

■

LAURENCE OLIVIER
1907—1989

British actor Olivier conquered Hollywood as Heath-cliff in *Wuthering Heights* and then remained a star in such varied works as *King Lear* and *The Entertainer*, and in such roles as the vicious drill-wielding Nazi dentist who torments Dustin Hoffman with the question "Is it safe?" in *Marathon Man*. Married to two extraordinary English actresses—first Vivien Leigh and later Joan Plowright—he was often regarded as the leader of a stellar group of his peers, a group that consisted of John Gielgud, John Mills, Ralph Richardson, and Michael Redgrave. Known as "Larry" to his friends, he had the uncanny ability to alter both his voice and his appearance in an astonishing variety of roles.

BURIED: Westminster Cathedral, London, England

FREDERICK LAW OLMSTED
1822—1903

The designer and builder of Central Park gained fame first as a travel writer, then later as a landscape architect. His best-selling books depicted the slaveholder society in the American South. His park designs, including those for Prospect Park in Brooklyn and parks in Montreal, Chicago, and Buffalo, were visionary. A century after they were built, they are just now being recognized as American treasures.

BURIED: Old North Cemetery, Hartford, Connecticut

■

ARISTOTLE ONASSIS
1906—1975

The Greek shipping magnate started his fortune by manufacturing a cigarette for women (who did not yet smoke) and then persuading a well-known opera singer to smoke one in public. It started a craze, and millions of women began smoking overnight, making Ari a millionaire. Years later he would become the lover of the most famous opera diva of all time, Maria Callas, a woman he abruptly abandoned to marry Jacqueline Kennedy. Because of the head-on collision of a fun-loving Greek and a New York socialite, this last marriage was an unhappy alliance; his family referred to her as "The Widow." When near death in a Paris hospital he drafted his last will and testament, leaving everything to his daughter, Christina; Jackie "O" was allegedly given millions when she agreed not to contest the will.

BURIED: The Chapel on Skorpios Island, Skorpios, Greece

■

EUGENE O'NEILL
1888—1953

Winner of the Pulitzer Prize in 1920 and the Nobel Prize for Literature in 1936, he was born the son of an actor, and before turning to playwriting was a seaman, a prospector, a derelict, and a newspaper reporter. His career began in Provincetown, Massachusetts, in a local theater and quickly moved to Broadway. His alcoholism and drug addiction finally destroyed him, but not before he wrote a body of work considered by a dwindling number of critics as the finest in the American theater.

BURIED: Forest Hills Cemetery, Boston, Massachusetts

ROY ORBISON
1936—1988

Originally a country-and-western singer, this strange-looking entertainer with the dark glasses, chalk-white skin, and black hair had a voice like an angel; he was unique, a complete original with an unforgettable voice. His success with hits like "Crying" and "Oh, Pretty Woman" was marred by tragedy in his personal life. Almost forgotten by a new generation of record buyers, his fame was resurrected just before his death when he joined Bob Dylan, George Harrison, Tom

Petty, and Jeff Lynne to form The Traveling Wilburys on an album that has become a modern classic.

BURIED: Westwood Village Memorial Park, Los Angeles, California

■

LEE HARVEY OSWALD
1939—1963

Alleged assassin (according to the much-disputed Warren Commission report) of President John F. "Where were you when he was shot?" Kennedy, he was the first person ever murdered on live television. His wife and parents were forced into litigation to gain his interment in the Oswald family plot.

BURIED: Rose Hill Cemetery, Fort Worth, Texas

■

JESSE OWENS
1913—1980

At the 1936 Olympic games in Berlin Owens upset Hitler's theory of Aryan superiority by winning four gold medals and setting three new world records.

BURIED: Olympics Oakwoods Cemetery, Chicago, Illinois

■

SATCHEL PAIGE
1906—1982

The second black player in baseball's major leagues, he once said, "Don't look back; somebody might be gaining on you."

BURIED: Forest Hills Cemetery, Kansas City, Missouri

■

BONNIE PARKER
1910—1934

She was the female half of Bonnie and Clyde, the famous duo who robbed banks and were immortalized on film. She actually bore some resemblance to Faye Dunaway, and dressed in the latest fashions, wrote poetry, and smoked cigars.

BURIED: Crown Hill Memorial Park (moved from Fish Trap Cemetery), West Dallas, Texas

■

CHARLIE PARKER
1920—1955

"Bird" died at the age of thirty-five in the apartment of the Baroness Nica de Koenigswarter, his health destroyed by drugs and alcohol. In his short lifetime he completely changed the course of jazz. The key figure in the Bebop revolution of the 1940s and the most imaginative player of his era, Parker introduced radical innovations in harmony and rhythm. His performances influenced a generation of younger players, and his recordings, although not recognized by critics when released, are now considered classics.

BURIED: Lincoln Cemetery, Kansas City, Missouri

DOROTHY PARKER
1893—1967

As the only female member of the fabled Algonquin round table, Parker was known as the wittiest woman in America, and her first collection of light verse, *Enough Rope*, was a best-seller for years. Ensconced at *The New Yorker* as a book reviewer whose byline was Constant Reader, she savaged as many books as she praised, ending a critique of a Winnie-the-Pooh book with the now-famous line, "Tonstant Weader frowed up." Born into a wealthy Jewish family in New York City—her surname was Rothschild—she rebelled against the nuns who educated her and tried to convert her to Roman Catholicism. A lifelong commitment to left-wing politics and civil rights became surprisingly apparent when she left her entire estate to the Rev. Martin Luther King, Jr., a man she had never met. Alcoholic and suicidal, her view of life was as bleak as Samuel Beckett's in spite of her fame as a wit. After her death her ashes were kept in a file cabinet for over twenty years at her lawyer's office; they were refused a place of honor by both *The New Yorker* and the Algonquin. In 1988 her remains found the perfect home.

CREMATED: Ashes interred at NAACP Headquarters, Baltimore, Maryland

■

LOUELLA PARSONS
1881—1972

Overweight and unattractive, this gossip columnist was rumored to have extracted a lifelong contract from William Randolph Hearst after she supposedly witnessed a murder aboard his yacht and then agreed to keep her mouth shut. The mere mention of an up-and-coming star in her column could often make or break a career; her power in Hollywood was unequaled during her reign of terror. The Queen of Gossip used this power maliciously toward those who would not bow to her demands.

BURIED: Holy Cross Cemetery, Culver City, California

■

PETEY

The all-white canine star of the Our Gang movies appeared in some films with a black ring painted around his right eye and in other films with the ring around his left eye.

BURIED: Hollywood Memorial Park, Los Angeles, California

■

EDITH PIAF
1915—1963

The "Little Sparrow" was raised in a bordello, hit the streets as a singer at the age of fifteen, lost her two-year-old daughter to meningitis, lost one lover and one husband in plane crashes, was badly hurt herself in three car accidents, developed painful rheumatism that crippled her, became addicted to morphine and alcohol, and garnered fanatical devotion from her fans. When she was buried, forty thousand people rioted at the cemetery. Her devotees still cover her grave with fresh flowers every day.

BURIED: Père Lachaise Cemetery, Paris, France

■

PABLO PICASSO
1881—1973

Perhaps the most influential artist of the twentieth century, he first gained recognition with *Les Demoiselles d'Avignon*, a painting that altered the course of art forever. He loathed Freud, either adored or hated women (he mutilated them in his work), was bisexual, self-aggrandizing, cruel to those he loved, and was indisputably one of the towering geniuses of the modern world, and he knew it. He once said, "My mother told me that if I had gone into politics, I would have been president, and if I had entered the Church, I would have become Pope. But I went into painting, and I became Picasso."

BURIED: The Garden at Notre-Dame-de-Vie, Vauve-
      nargues, France

HORACE PIPPIN
1888—1946

While serving with a Negro battalion in the U.S. Army, his right hand was wounded, and Pippin was discharged. He returned home, married a woman with several children, and started to paint. It took him three years to finish his first picture, and several years later he was discovered by a New York gallery of folk art. His fame was immediate and secure.

BURIED: Chestnut Grove Annex Cemetery, West
      Chester, Pennsylvania

ZASU PITTS
1900—1963

This actress began her career as a serious dramatic star in films like *Greed* but later developed a scatter-brained character for films like *Life with Father* and *It's a Mad Mad Mad Mad World*.

BURIED: Holy Cross Cemetery, Culver City, California

■

POPE PIUS XII
1876—1958

The first pope to become known, examined, and even criticized by the media, he served as his own secretary of state in the Vatican, altering the traditions of the church by limiting the role of the cardinals, thereby making his own position more powerful. During World War II he refused to criticize the Nazi Party or denounce Hitler's persecution of the Jews.

BURIED: Saint Peter's, Vatican City, Rome, Italy

■

SYLVIA PLATH
1932—1963

This American poet was born in Boston and committed suicide in her London kitchen. At the time of her death she had published only one book of poems and a novel, *The Bell Jar*. Recognized posthumously, her poetry is sometimes witty and affectionate, but most often it deals with emotional pain. More than that of any other American poet, her cult following continues to grow.

BURIED: Parish Churchyard, Heptonsall, Yorkshire, England

POCAHONTAS
1595—1617

She was the daughter of the chief of the Powhatan Indians in Virginia, and it is said she saved the life of Captain John Smith. Forced to convert to Christianity and marry a different John (John Rolfe), she and her husband traveled to England, where she was received as royalty. Unfortunately, only John returned to Virginia; Pocahontas, the Indian princess, died on board ship.

BURIED: St. George's Churchyard, Gravesend, England

EDGAR ALLAN POE
1809—1849

With the publication of "Murders in the Rue Morgue"
Poe invented the modern detective story. His work
influenced everyone from Baudelaire (who did the first
French translations) to Freud and Sartre. This American genius was born in Boston to actor parents who
left him an orphan. He was then taken into the household of a tobacco exporter in Richmond, Virginia. Poe
studied in England and at the University of Virginia,
where he incurred huge gambling debts and was forced
to leave. After publishing his first collection of verse
at his own expense, he joined the Army. Dishonorably
discharged from West Point, he turned to a career in
journalism and married his thirteen-year-old cousin.
The publication of "The Raven" in a New York paper
brought him fame, but he died penniless from alcoholism after being discovered delirious, living on the
streets of Baltimore.

BURIED: Westminster Presbyterian Church, Baltimore, Maryland

JACKSON POLLOCK
1912—1956

This macho American painter, who caught the public's
eye after *Time* magazine called him Jack the Dripper,

developed a method of working called action painting. Critics, dealers, and collectors went wild. His work helped change the direction of twentieth-century art, but unfortunately success and the wealth it brought were too much for Pollock to handle. His drinking became pathological and his reckless behavior extravagant. He killed himself in a car crash while drunk at the wheel.

BURIED: Green River Cemetery, East Hampton, Long Island, New York

■

COLE PORTER
1891—1964

One of the most prolific songwriters in American musical history, he wrote such classics as "Night and Day," "You're the Top," "I Get a Kick Out of You" and "Begin the Beguine." In addition, he created such Broadway hits as *Kiss Me Kate*, *Anything Goes*, and *Silk Stockings*. The epitome of stylish sophistication, he partied all night, drank champagne, had endless affairs (allegedly including one with "Black Jack" Bouvier, Jackie O's dad), slept late, and threw orgies in his fabulous suite at the Waldorf-Astoria in New York City. After falling from a horse, he remained crippled for the rest of his life, and his leg was amputated in 1958. Despite his failing health, he attempted to maintain his glamorous image and life-style, which included daily visits from muscular masseurs, elegant dinner parties, morning haircuts, and trips to Hollywood. As his condition worsened, the whirl of parties slowed to a standstill, and he soon lost interest in seeing even his closest friends. He died a virtual recluse.

BURIED: Mount Hope Cemetery, Peru, Indiana

■

EZRA POUND
1885—1972

The controversy that surrounded the American poet Pound obscured for many years the quality of his work. During World War II he made anti-Semitic broadcasts for the Italian government and in 1945 was arrested for treason. He was sent back to the United States, found mentally unfit to stand trial, and was placed in a sanitorium until his release in 1958. After he returned to Italy his reputation soared, and today he is widely considered the master of traditional verse form and the artist who modernized poetry.

BURIED: Isola di San Michele, Venice, Italy

ADAM CLAYTON POWELL, JR.
1908—1972

The New York congressman from Harlem proposed more civil rights legislation than any other person in American history and is considered to be the architect of Lyndon Johnson's "Great Society." He retreated to the island of Bimini after being hounded out of Congress by colleagues who knew he had been unjustly accused of a crime.

CREMATED: Ashes scattered over Bimini

ELEANOR POWELL
1912—1982

Fred Astaire called her "the greatest tap dancer of all time," but unfortunately her ability to act did not quite measure up to her dancing. Films like *Born to Dance* and *Broadway Melody of 1938* were successful simply because of her inspired feet, and after divorcing Glenn Ford, she forged a career in nightclubs, tapping her toes until she died of cancer.

BURIED: Hollywood Memorial Park, Los Angeles, California

■

TYRONE POWER
1914—1958

Tyrone Power was one of those handsome leading men who graduated from swashbuckling roles into a performer of substance in such films as *The Razor's Edge* and *Witness for the Prosecution*. During World War II he served the country as a marine. After returning to Hollywood, he died an untimely death at age forty-four from a heart attack.

BURIED: Hollywood Memorial Park, Los Angeles, California

■

ELVIS PRESLEY
1935—1977

The white granddaddy of rock 'n roll, sometimes known as "The King," swiveled his hips at a comatose nation during the late 1950s and brought blue suede shoes and hound dogs into the general vernacular. Slim, good looking, and blessed with a way with a song, he spent the last years of his life overweight, addicted to drugs, and dressed like a clown. Singing Las Vegas–style to the faithful who had grown up on his music, he continued to mesmerize those who refused to acknowledge his visible problems. The persona he created has spawned a plethora of imitators all over the globe. Some people even think he is not dead but happily eating at a Burger King in Kalamazoo.

BURIED: Graceland, Memphis, Tennessee

■

FREDDIE PRINZE
1954—1977

Born in New York City, this Puerto Rican comedian, who was actually half Hungarian, was the star of "Chico and the Man," a situation comedy that had an audience of millions. Young, brash, and addicted to Quaaludes, he had an unhealthy fascination with death and was obsessed with Lenny Bruce. Fond of repeatedly watching tapes of the assassination of John F.

Kennedy, few of his friends were surprised when he committed suicide by shooting himself in the head.

BURIED: Forest Lawn Hollywood Hills, Los Angeles, California

■

MARCEL PROUST
1871–1922

A true Parisian, Proust wrote *Remembrance of Things Past*, a voluminous novel that many consider the finest book ever written. He lived in relative isolation, receiving visitors in bed. He was a chronic hypochondriac and a great wit. When told that the woman he loved was not pretty, he replied, "Let's leave the pretty women to the men without imagination."

BURIED: Père Lachaise Cemetery, Paris, France

■

SERGEI RACHMANINOFF
1873–1943

Born into an aristocratic family, Rachmaninoff fled Russia on the day before the Revolution of 1917. He suffered a severe depression early in his career and took up self-hypnosis in order to compose. In the

United States he was celebrated as a performer more than a composer, and although his music was scorned by the critics, it has found a secure place in the hearts of his many fans.

BURIED: Kensico Cemetery, Valhalla, New York

■

GEORGE RAFT
1895—1980

Barred from England for operating an illegal gambling club, "tough guy" Raft started in show business as a dancer before he made movies like *Each Dawn I Die* and *Some Like It Hot*. His public persona mirrored his actual relationships with gangsters like Al Capone and Bugsy Siegel, and although he boasted about his many affairs with starlets like Grable, Lombard, and Monroe, there are those who insist he preferred masculine partners more.

BURIED: Forest Lawn Hollywood Hills, Los Angeles, California

■

MA RAINEY
1886—1939

Gertrude Pridgett grew up to become Ma Rainey, "Mother of the Blues," the first of the great women blues singers. She discovered Bessie Smith and took the young singer under her wing, touring with the Rabbit Foot Minstrels. After recording over ninety records with people like Louis Armstrong, Fletcher Henderson, and Coleman Hawkins, she left show business in 1928. Fate was good to her; she retired a wealthy woman and the owner of two theaters.

BURIED: Porterdale Cemetery, Columbus, Georgia

CLAUDE RAINS
1889—1963

After a successful career on the English stage, Rains came to American films and never stopped giving unforgettable performances. He tricked our minds in *The Invisible Man*, ignited our imaginations in *The Adventures of Robin Hood*, had us screaming in *The Phantom of the Opera*, made us laugh in *Casablanca*, and broke our hearts in *Mr. Skeffington*.

BURIED: Red Hill Cemetery, Moultonboro, New Hampshire

AYN RAND
1905—1982

Born in St. Petersburg, Russia, this writer thought of herself as a philosopher. She championed a way of thinking she called Objectivism, and became famous for two novels, *The Fountainhead* and *Atlas Shrugged*. Totally opposed to any form of charity, Rand's philosophy is still popular with some greedy and egotistical seekers of the American dream. Thwarted in love in her private life, this passionate capitalist died of lung cancer alone and without friends.

BURIED: Kensico Cemetery, Valhalla, New York

SALLY RAND
1904—1979

H. L. Mencken coined the term "ecdysiast" to describe Sally Rand, the greatest stripteaser of all time. Born Helen Gould Beck, she took her name from the atlas and promptly undressed at the 1933 World's Fair. She was arrested for indecent exposure, and from that moment on the creator of the famous fan dance was a star.

BURIED: Oakdale Memorial Park, Glendale, California

BASIL RATHBONE
1892—1967

"It's elementary, my dear Watson" is, much to his regret, the line most closely associated with Basil Rathbone. To his fans he *is* Sherlock Holmes. Born in South Africa and educated in London, he made over seventy movies after moving to the United States. Most of these film roles are completely forgotten, but as the Baker Street detective he will remain firmly fixed in the pantheon of cultural icons.

BURIED: Ferncliff Mausoleum, Hartsdale, New York

■

MAURICE RAVEL
1875—1937

The French composer of Basque descent moved to Paris when he was only three months old and began composing while still in his teens. His composition *Bolero*, which he described as "a piece for orchestra without music," is one of the most well-known pieces of music in the world.

BURIED: Levallois Cemetery, Paris, France

■

DONNA REED
1921—1986

The sultry costar of *From Here to Eternity* (for which she won an Oscar) is best known for her role as the archetypal American mother on "The Donna Reed Show."

BURIED: Westwood Memorial Park, Los Angeles, California

■

JOHN REED
1887—1920

Reed was an American communist who used his family fortune to support the Russian Revolution of 1917, which he chronicled in the book *Ten Days That Shook the World*. From Seattle to New York City and from Provincetown to the Soviet Union, he was an ardent spokesperson for the Party. His life was Hollywood-ized in Warren Beatty's film *Reds*.

BURIED: The Kremlin Wall, Moscow, USSR

■

GEORGE REEVES
1914—1959

When television's Superman committed suicide and his nude body was discovered in his Los Angeles bedroom, his young fans lost some of their innocence. The six-foot two-inch tall actor had been so firmly fixed in the minds of the public as the caped superhero that he was continually rejected for any other role. In despair he shot himself in the head with a .30-caliber Luger pistol.

BURIED: Forest Lawn, Glendale, California

■

REMBRANDT VAN RIJN
1606—1669

Everyone knows this Dutch painter's most famous painting, *The Night Watch*, an enormous canvas that has withstood attacks from madmen wielding knives and solvents. Fabulously successful in his own lifetime, he squandered his money, piled up huge debts, and died penniless. Primarily appreciated for his portraiture, he was not averse to displaying the kind of humor that often repelled his audience and once exhibited an etching called The Good Samaritan that featured a dog emptying his bowels in the street.

BURIED: Unmarked grave, Westerkerk, Amsterdam, The Netherlands

■

RIN TIN TIN

One of the biggest box-office stars of all time, Rin Tin Tin was an Alsatian sheepdog who wowed his fans by coming to the rescue in dozens of silent films. This wonder dog saved not only lives but also his studio—from bankruptcy—and spawned a pack of imitators.

BURIED: At the home of his trainer, Los Angeles, California

■

DIEGO RIVERA
1886—1957

Considered by many to be the founder of modern Mexican painting, Rivera was one of the three artists (along with José Orozco and David Siqueiros) who dominated the legendary Mexican mural movement. His monumental mural *Man at the Crossroads* at Rockefeller Center in New York City was destroyed by John D. Rockefeller because of its leftist political content but was repainted by the artist in Mexico City.

BURIED: Rotonda de los Hombres Ilustres, Mexico City, Mexico

■

PAUL ROBESON
1898—1976

Writer, linguist, athlete, orator, singer, and actor, he popularized the song "Old Man River" in the movie *Showboat* and became a major force in American theater and politics. He was the son of a slave and became an American hero of mythic proportions. Unjustly pursued by the right-wing zealots of the House Un-American Activities Committee for both his leftist leanings and his sexual prowess, he was nevertheless loved by the world community. He was continually harassed by the U.S. government until his tragic death.

BURIED: Ferncliff Cemetery, Hartsdale, New York

■

BILL "BOJANGLES" ROBINSON
1878—1949

Known throughout America as the greatest tap dancer in the world, this African-American vaudeville star became a Broadway staple before moving on to Hollywood films, the most famous of which is *Rebecca of Sunnybrook Farm* with Shirley Temple. He also set a world record for running backwards.

BURIED: Evergreen Cemetery, Brooklyn, New York

■

EDWARD G. ROBINSON
1893—1973

His performance as a gangster in countless films (*Little Caesar* and *Key Largo*, to name only two) became the model for real-life hoodlums. In reality he was a generous philanthropist and a cultured gentleman, who amassed a serious international art collection.

BURIED: Beth-El Cemetery, Westchester, New York

JACKIE ROBINSON
1919—1972

This African-American baseball player broke the color barrier in the major leagues. One of the fastest runners in the game, he stoically endured the racist abuse of both white baseball fans and his own teammates. With his wife, Rachel, beside him he refused to retaliate against his attackers, and his dignity and courage made him a folk-hero long before the emergence of the nonviolent civil rights movement of Dr. Martin Luther King, Jr.

BURIED: Cypress Hills Cemetery, Westchester, New York

NELSON ROCKEFELLER
1908—1979

New York governor and vice-president of the U.S. under Gerald Ford, he died "in the saddle" with his secretary. Born into one of America's wealthiest families—his father John D. was the oil baron who exploited poor laborers—Nelson came to power as a Republican in an overwhelmingly Democratic New York State and then used his position as governor to run for the presidency but failed. An avid art collector, he was also a philanthropist who nurtured the arts in America and was married to a woman named Happy.

BURIED: Pocantico, Tarrytown, New York

■

NORMAN ROCKWELL
1894—1978

Famous for his anecdotal scenes of white middle-class American life, Norman Rockwell achieved incredible success as an illustrator. His covers for *The Saturday Evening Post* reflected the way most Americans viewed their nation, but the innocuous portrait he painted was shattered by the realities of the 1960s.

BURIED: Stockbridge Cemetery, Stockbridge, Massachusetts

■

AUGUSTE RODIN
1840—1917

Probably the most famous sculptor of all time, his work, especially *The Thinker* and *The Kiss*, has been copied in miniatures made of plastic, metal, and even chocolate. Near the end of his life he was hounded by the French government for what they saw as his anti-Christian stance, and he was forced to spend his final year painting and drawing instead of sculpting. He married his long-suffering mistress just two weeks before she died and ten months before his own demise. The French government finally changed its hostile attitude and created the Musée Rodin, housing a collection that stands as a testament to this great artist's genius.

BURIED: Villa des Brilliants, Paris, France

■

ELEANOR ROOSEVELT
1884—1962

This ugly duckling of the Roosevelt family married her cousin Franklin and became the greatest first lady the nation has ever known. She tirelessly campaigned for her husband's election as president, acting not only as his right hand but also his legs; their relationship was a partnership more than a marriage. They were both greatly loved by the people whom they served. Mrs.

Roosevelt, linked romantically to her female secretary, was a passionate spokesperson for those who had little or no voice in government.

BURIED: Franklin Delano Roosevelt National Historic Site, Hyde Park, New York

■

THEODORE ROOSEVELT
1858—1919

The man who inspired the teddy bear was a man of great contradictions and mood swings. He won the Nobel Peace Prize for negotiating peace between Russia and Japan but believed in "walking softly and carrying a big stick," the big stick being a fleet of battleships sent to Panama to help start a revolution so that the United States could build the canal. He was a wild-game hunter who once killed 468 animals on a single safari, yet he set aside millions of acres of land for national parks. A writer, soldier, cowboy, politician, naturalist, policeman, and explorer, he apparently suffered from manic depression.

BURIED: Young's Memorial Cemetery, Oyster Bay, Long Island, New York

■

ETHEL ROSENBERG
1915—1953

JULIUS ROSENBERG
1918—1953

Whether they were innocent victims of cold-war hysteria combined with anti-Semitism or guilty spies who passed national secrets to the Soviets, their execution remains at the center of a controversy that still rages.

BURIED: Wellwood Cemetery, Farmingdale, Long Island, New York

■

BETSY ROSS
1752—1836

Sorry, but Betsy Ross, although she was most definitely a seamstress in Philadelphia and did sew flags during the Revolutionary War, did *not* design and make the first American flag.

BURIED: Mount Moria Cemetery, Philadelphia, Pennsylvania

■

MARK ROTHKO
1903—1970

When this chronically depressed but brilliant abstract painter slashed his elbows and bled to death on the floor of his studio, he left behind hundreds of paintings worth millions of dollars. His executors sold the paintings for less than market value to the Marlboro Gallery, which then sold them for their true value. The subsequent legal battle lasted six years, with the gallery owners and the executors ultimately losing. Together they had to pay fines of over 9 million dollars, and the paintings, worth 30 million, were turned over to Rothko's daughter.

BURIED: East Marion Cemetery, East Marion, Long
     Island, New York

■

JACK RUBY
1911—1967

Born Jack Rubenstein, this Dallas businessman owned a local striptease joint before he became one of the most famous men in the United States for gunning down Lee Harvey Oswald in front of seventy policemen and millions of stunned television viewers. Convicted of murder and sentenced to death, he died of cancer before he could be executed.

BURIED: West Lawn Cemetery, Chicago, Illinois

■

ROSALIND RUSSELL
1908—1976

Her many portrayals of liberated women, such as
Amelia Earhart and Sister Kenny, long before fem-
inism surfaced in the cinema, led to one of the great
roles of her life as Auntie Mame. Known as Roz to her
many friends, she danced her way through *My Sister
Eileen* and gave the boys a run for their money in *His
Girl Friday*. One of her few attempts at serious drama,
in Eugene O'Neill's *Mourning Becomes Electra*, was
a major disaster. Crippled with arthritis in her later
years, she became a philanthropist and left a legacy
of laughter that will live forever, showing her audiences (to paraphrase Auntie Mame) "worlds they
never dreamed existed."

BURIED: Holy Cross Cemetery, Culver City, California

■

BABE RUTH
1894—1948

Probably the most famous of all American sports heroes, Babe defined baseball. He began his career in
the major leagues with the Boston Red Sox, a team
he led to the World Series. Sold to the Yankees (a
blow to the Sox from which they have yet to recover),
his career changed baseball history forever. With a
salary higher than that of President Hoover, he played

until he was almost unable to walk and died two months after his final game.

BURIED: Gate of Heaven Cemetery, Mt. Pleasant, New York

■

SABU
1924—1963

||||||||||||||||||||||||||||||||||||||||||||||||||||||||||||||||||||||||||||||||||||||||||||||||||||||||||||||||||||||||||||||||||||||||||||||||||||||||||

Plucked from the back of an elephant in his native India, Sabu Dastigar was flown to Hollywood and made into a star in such films as *The Jungle Book* and *Song of India*.

BURIED: Forest Lawn Hollywood Hills, Los Angeles, California

■

SACCO & VANZETTI
NICOLA SACCO
1891—1927

BARTOLOMEO VANZETTI
1888—1927

Falsely arrested for murder, these passionate anarchists were tried, found guilty, and executed for their political beliefs, causing worldwide demonstrations on their behalf.

BURIED: Turin, Italy

■

DIANA SANDS
1934—1973

This beautiful and talented African-American actress reached the pinnacle of her success as the young woman who wants to become a doctor in *A Raisin in the Sun*, a role she originated on Broadway and repeated on the screen. She also appeared on stage in two first plays by distinguished American writers, in James Baldwin's *Blues for Mister Charlie* and Joseph Heller's *We Bombed in New Haven*.

BURIED: Ferncliff Cemetery, Hartsdale, New York

■

MARGARET HIGGINS SANGER
1883—1966

Her work as a nurse convinced Sanger that birth control was necessary for social progress, and her subsequent promotion of contraception landed her in jail.

BURIED: Rural Cemetery, Fishkill, New York

■

JEAN-PAUL SARTRE
1905—1980

He was France's most impassioned practitioner of atheistic existentialism and its loudest voice. Author of the seminal *Being and Nothingness*, he advanced the concept that man is nothing more than the sum of his past, with each individual starting from nothing and creating a life. In short, he thought that humans are "condemned to be free."

BURIED: Montparnasse Cemetery, Paris, France

■

JEAN SEBERG
1938—1979

Born in America, she became a cult figure in Europe for her role in the film *Breathless* opposite Jean-Paul Belmondo. She later attracted a great deal of bad press when she became an activist for the Black Panther Party. Her body was discovered in a parked car, and the cause of death remains a mystery.

BURIED: Montparnasse Cemetery, Paris, France

■

EDIE SEDGWICK
1943—1971

Born into one of New England's most prestigious families and raised on a vast and isolated California ranch, she became a "superstar" during the 1960s as the "Girl of the Year" in the New York Underground. Both despised and adored by people like Truman Capote, Norman Mailer, Gore Vidal, Andy Warhol, and Bob Dylan (who supposedly wrote "Visions of Johanna" about her), Edie became a symbol of self-destruction, sex, drugs, and rock and roll. Her film credits include *Ciao Manhattan*, a Warholean nightmare that managed to survive even though a dog ate the original negative.

BURIED: Oak Hill Cemetery, Ballard, California

■

DAVID O. SELZNICK
1902—1965

He belonged to the rare breed of independent Hollywood producers and gave the world such classics as *Gone with the Wind, Rebecca, Spellbound, The Third Man,* and *A Farewell to Arms.*

BURIED: Forest Lawn, Glendale, California

■

ROD SERLING
1924—1975

From 1959 to 1963 Rod Serling's "Twilight Zone" thrilled its fans. The series was never a ratings success, but it influenced the next generation of makers of television programs and films. Although he had had several earlier successes as a scriptwriter with *Requiem for a Heavyweight* and *Patterns,* he never received the critical respect he wanted and died a broken man.

BURIED: Interlaken Cemetery, Interlaken, New York

■

GEORGE BERNARD SHAW
1856—1950

The Irish writer, whose plays expressed his passionate belief in socialism, and who also wrote novels and nonfiction, won the Nobel Prize in 1925. A severe critic of Christianity, puritanism, and poverty (which he called the cause of all evil) Shaw consistently challenged the moral predicaments mankind creates for itself. A prolific writer, his plays include *Major Barbara, Man and Superman* and *Arms and the Man*, but he is best known for his play *Pygmalion*, which was the basis for the musical *My Fair Lady*. He was a strict vegetarian; never drank alcoholic beverages, coffee, or tea; and lived to be ninety-four.

CREMATED: Ashes interred, Golders Green, London, England

■

NORMA SHEARER
1900—1983

Married to Irving Thalberg, the head honcho at MGM, Shearer was transformed by her powerful husband into a first-rate star in such films as *Strange Interlude* and *The Barretts of Wimpole Street*. After her husband's death she made some unwise career moves (like turning down the title role in *Mrs. Miniver* because she did not want to play the mother of a grown son) and retired from the screen after marrying her ski instructor, a man twenty years her junior.

BURIED: (with Irving Thalberg) Forest Lawn, Glendale, California

■

BISHOP FULTON J. SHEEN
1895—1977

The first radio evangelist (on "The Catholic Hour"), he turned his talent to television and managed to attract over 20 million loyal fans, much to the surprise of the network executives. Dressed in his elaborate church vestments, he was the charismatic host of "Life Is Worth Living," a television show that denounced communism and Freudian analysis among other things. During his career he converted many famous people to Catholicism, including Clare Boothe Luce and Henry Ford II.

BURIED: St. Patrick's Cathedral, New York, New York

■

PERCY BYSSHE SHELLEY
1792—1822

"Mad Shelley" so outraged his fellow Englishmen with his ideas on free love and atheism that he was forced to leave England and live in Italy. His death at the age of thirty occurred at sea. Three days later his body washed ashore and was buried in the sand until it was removed and cremated. A friend snatched Shelley's heart out of the cremation fire and mailed it to his widow, Mary Shelley, the author of *Frankenstein*.

CREMATED: Ashes buried in the Protestant Cemetery, Rome, Italy

BUGSY SIEGEL
1906—1947

Although he was a close friend of Clark Gable, Abbott and Costello, and other Hollywood stars, this gangster led a double life as a homosexual and as a member of "Murder Inc." He was the head of the mob on the West Coast, helped start Las Vegas, controlled the heroin traffic from Mexico, and was suspected of several murders. He was shot to death through a window as he sat on the couch in his Beverly Hills home.

BURIED: Beth O'lam Hollywood Memorial Park, Hollywood, California

KAREN SILKWOOD
1946—1974

After planning to expose the health hazards that existed in the nuclear reactor factory where she worked in Oklahoma, she was mysteriously killed while on her way to meet with a reporter. Her death was officially regarded as an accident, but her report was missing from the car, and murder seems logical. The case prompted Congress to investigate the very problems she was attempting to expose, and her family sued the company she worked for all the way to the Supreme Court, winning a judgment for 10 million dollars (they later settled out of court for less than 2 million). Her life was made into a film called *Silkwood* starring Meryl Streep in the title role.

BURIED: Danville Cemetery, Kilgore, Texas

■

PHIL SILVERS
1911—1985

After starting out in vaudeville and appearing on Broadway in *Top Banana*, Silvers's name became a household word in the television series "You'll Never Get Rich" playing Sergeant Bilko. His film roles were always supporting, but he was unforgettable in *You're in the Army Now* and *A Funny Thing Happened on the Way to the Forum*.

BURIED: Mt. Sinai Memorial Park, Los Angeles, California

■

SITTING BULL
1831—1890

General Custer was defeated at the Little Bighorn in
1876 by Indian forces led by the great Chief Sitting
Bull. Unfortunately it was only a minor victory against
the white man's genocidal campaign to drive the Sioux
onto reservations. Sitting Bull toured briefly with the
Buffalo Bill Wild West Show but returned to the res-
ervation, where he began the Ghost Dance Movement,
a revival of ancient tribal rituals that helped solidify
Indian resistance to white oppression. He was unarmed when shot and killed by an Indian police officer.

BURIED: Sitting Bull Monument, Mobridge, South
Dakota

EDDIE SLOVIK
1920—1945

This young man had the bad luck to be the only American soldier executed for desertion during World
War II.

BURIED: American Cemetery, Seringes-sur-Nesles,
France

BESSIE SMITH
1894—1937

The "Empress of the Blues" was born in Chattanooga, Tennessee, and grew up singing in church. At the age of fourteen she began singing with Ma Rainey and the Rabbit Foot Minstrels. She is responsible for bringing the blues out of southern vaudeville and into the mainstream of pop culture. Her recordings remain a legacy that continues to influence contemporary vocal styles. Ever since her fatal injury in a car crash a legend has persisted that places responsibility for her subsequent death on the refusal of a whites-only hospital to admit her. The truth may never be known, but until 1970 she lay in an unmarked grave. Janis Joplin and Smith's former maid paid for a monument placed on her grave which reads, "The Greatest Blues Singer in the World Will Never Stop Singing."

BURIED: Mt. Lawn Cemetery, Sharon Hill, Pennsylvania

■

KATE SMITH
1919—1986

An American icon for generations, her rendition of "God Bless America" became the standard by which all others were judged. Terribly overweight and completely self-taught, she sang her way into the homes and hearts of her native land by belting out "When the Moon Comes Over the Mountain," her signature piece, which she never failed to perform at every concert she gave. Her will stipulated that she not be buried underground, and after years of haggling an above-ground crypt was erected and her enormous body finally laid to rest.

BURIED: Lake Placid Cemetery, Lake Placid, New York

■

SMOKEY THE BEAR

Yes, Virginia, there really was a Smokey the Bear. He was actually a bear cub whose charred body was discovered after a forest fire in Montana.

BURIED: Smokey Bear Historical State Park, Captin, Montana

■

CHAIM SOUTINE
1893—1943

A Russian-born Jewish painter, Soutine spent his adult life in Paris as a contemporary of the most famous artists of the twentieth century, who were developing Cubism, Fauvism, and a host of other isms. Painfully shy and incredibly independent, he was determined to follow the dictates of his own soul rather than join a movement. His first heroes were Courbet and Rembrandt. Passionate almost to the point of madness, his work as well as his life is rightly compared to Van Gogh's, whose canvases look ordered compared to Soutine's chaotic and fantastic creations, which include lopsided landscapes, tortured portraits, and agonizingly vibrant animal carcasses. His long years of poverty ended when Dr. Barnes, an American collector, bought seventy-five canvases. But like Van Gogh, his mad passion and depression continued until his death from a perforated ulcer, which he had ignored. This final act, similar to suicide, capped the life of one of the most tortured and creative artists in history.

BURIED: Montparnasse Cemetery, Paris, France

■

FRANCIS CARDINAL SPELLMAN
1889—1967

The politically powerful Roman Catholic cardinal ruled with both an iron fist and a limp wrist from St. Patrick's Cathedral in New York City during the sexual revolution of the 1960s. A staunch supporter and friend of Senator Joe McCarthy and a hawk on Vietnam, he advocated the censorship of films he personally disapproved of. Outwardly effete and rumored to be gay, he was once introduced to Tallulah Bankhead, who remarked, "Darling, I love your dress, but your handbag's on fire."

BURIED: St. Patrick's Cathedral, New York, New York

■

JOSEPH STALIN
1879—1953

The son of a shoemaker, Stalin embraced Marxism and was often sent to prison. Escaping just as often, even from Siberia, he was finally released after the Revolution of 1917 and became a close ally of Lenin for several years. After Lenin's death he became the dictator of the USSR. During his murderous reign he industrialized the country (and in the process impoverished it), signed nonaggression pacts with most of his European neighbors, joined the Allies against Germany, met with Churchill and Roosevelt, and slaughtered millions of his own people.

BURIED: First interred next to Lenin, Red Square, Moscow, USSR (later removed; whereabouts unknown)

■

BARBARA STANWYCK
1907—1990

Little Ruby Stevens was four when her mother was murdered, and she was abandoned by her father. She left Brooklyn as soon as she was able and moved to Hollywood, changing her name to Barbara Stanwyck. She excelled in films as a tough-talking, self-sufficient woman with a tender heart. Famous for her roles in *Stella Dallas* and *Double Indemnity* (for which she received two of her four Oscar nominations), she never actually won the award, but in 1944 she was the highest-paid woman in America. In the mid-1960s she became a television star in "The Big Valley."

CREMATED: Ashes scattered over the Pacific Ocean

■

GERTRUDE STEIN
1874—1946

A giant of modernism, she was born in Oakland ("there is no there there"), California, moved to France, and never returned, except to visit. Her influence on twentieth-century Western culture was enormous. She told Hemingway how to write and Picasso how to paint. Her home at 27 Rue de Fleurs in Paris was a Mecca to writers, musicians, and painters for two generations. Except for *The Making of Americans* and *The Autobiography of Alice B. Toklas*, her own work is largely unreadable in spite of the fact that she once remarked, "There are only three Jewish geniuses. Christ, Spinoza and myself."

BURIED: Père Lachaise Cemetery, Paris, France

■

JOHN STEINBECK
1902—1968

By the time this native Californian won the Nobel Prize for Literature in 1962, his reputation in the United States had sunk significantly. However, there can be no doubt that his novel *The Grapes of Wrath* is one of the great creations of American culture. Many of his novels, such as *East of Eden*, *Of Mice and Men*, *Tortilla Flat*, and *Travels with Charlie*, have been made into films and remain popular with the reading public.

CREMATED: Ashes scattered over the Pacific Ocean, monument located in the Garden of Memories Cemetery, Salinas, California

■

MAX STEINER
1888—1971

The Austrian composer was one of Hollywood's most talented and prolific film score writers, proving himself time and time again in such classics as *Gone with the Wind*, *Now Voyager*, *A Star Is Born*, and *Casablanca*. Bette Davis, after shooting her incredible death scene in *Dark Victory*, was assured that Steiner would not be doing the film. "Good," she replied, "his music would have me dead before I got to the top of the stairs."

BURIED: Forest Lawn, Glendale, California

■

HARRIET BEECHER STOWE
1811—1896

A Cincinnati schoolteacher, she furthered the abolitionist cause by writing *Uncle Tom's Cabin*. Originally published in serial form in the magazine *National Era*, the antislavery novel was a huge success when it appeared as a book in 1852. At the time it stirred up public sentiment against slavery and its many cruelties, but over the years the attitude toward the story and its characters has changed and the expression "Uncle Tom" is now pejorative.

BURIED: Andover Chapel Cemetery, Phillips Academy, Andover, Massachusetts

DOROTHY STRATTEN
1960—1980

A beautiful *Playboy* centerfold and an aspiring actress, her short career was ended when she was brutally raped and murdered by her deranged husband, who then killed himself. Bob Fosse directed a film of her life called *Star 80*.

BURIED: Westwood Memorial Park, Los Angeles, California

LEVI STRAUSS
1830—1902

Not the inventor of the wheel but the brains behind the most egalitarian article of clothing ever created, Strauss emigrated from Germany to the United States at the age of fourteen and headed to San Francisco, where he sold clothing to prospectors of the gold rush who were in need of tough pants. He stole the idea of the copper rivets (which strengthened the pockets) from another tailor but then chose a new sailcloth from Nîmes, France, and colored it with cheap indigo dye. Strauss adopted the style from trousers worn by Genoese sailors (who were called Genes), and it wasn't until after World War II that they became known to the rest of the world as "jeans"; in the 1960s they became the most universal garment in history.

BURIED: Home of Peace Cemetery, Colma, California

■

IGOR STRAVINSKY
1882—1971

The man who said, "My music is best understood by children and animals," was a musical giant. He was born in Russia, became first a French citizen, then an American citizen. He changed the face of contemporary music; while in Paris he composed avant-garde ballet music for Diaghilev. Audiences rioted when they heard *Le Sacre du Printemps* for the first time, thus ensuring Stravinsky's place in history. After he came to the United States, he completed his first opera, *The Rake's Progress*, with a libretto by W. H. Auden. His last composition, written at the age of eighty-four for his wife, was a setting for piano and voice of Edward Lear's "The Owl and the Pussycat."

BURIED: Isola di San Michele, Venice, Italy

ROBERT STROUD
1890—1963

While serving time in prison, Stroud became an ornithologist of some renown, and his life story was made into a Burt Lancaster film called *The Birdman of Alcatraz*.

BURIED: Masonic Cemetery, Metropolis, Illinois

ED SULLIVAN
1901—1974

Perhaps the most famous variety-show host in the history of television, he introduced American audiences to a countless number of future stars, such as the Beatles and Elvis Presley, often mispronouncing their names.

BURIED: Ferncliff Mausoleum, Hartsdale, New York

■

HERBERT TARNOWER
1910—1980

The Scarsdale Diet made this doctor and ladies' man a small fortune, but his name became a household word when his former lover Jean Harris murdered him in a crime of passion.

BURIED: Mt. Hope Cemetery, Hastings, New York

■

SHARON TATE
1943—1969

Married to the Polish film director Roman Polanski, she will never be forgotten because she was one of those killed by the Manson Family on one of their murderous rampages. It is difficult to tell from her performances in *Valley of the Dolls* and *Invasion of the Fearless Vampire Killers* whether her career in films ever would have flourished.

BURIED: Holy Cross Cemetery, Culver City, California

■

IRVING THALBERG
1899—1936

The "Boy Wonder" at MGM was one of the most successful producers in Hollywood, saving Louis B. Mayer from financial ruin during the Great Depression. A sickly, slight man, his ambition and quest for power were second only to his love for Norma Shearer. His death at age thirty-seven shattered his wife's career.

BURIED: (with Norma Shearer) Forest Lawn, Glendale, California

■

DYLAN THOMAS
1914—1953

The Welsh poet and playwright, whose best-known lines are "Do not go gentle into that good night. Rage, rage, against the dying of the light," was consumed by alcoholism for most of his adult life. He died drunk on a visit to New York City, where he was overseeing rehearsals of *Under Milkwood*, his masterwork. Caitlin, his wife and the mother of his three children, brought Dylan's body back to Wales by ship, with the poet's body stored below deck, a spot that suited her mood since she could sleep next to the coffin while deckhands drank beer and played cards on its lid.

BURIED: St. Martin's Churchyard, Laugharne, Wales

■

WILLIAM "BUCKWHEAT" THOMAS
1931—1980

One of the stars of the "Our Gang" comedies, Thomas used his great charm to transcend the racial stereotype of his Buckwheat persona, and in so doing, he managed to create a memorable and much-loved character.

Since his death, at least two impostors have claimed to be the real Buckwheat.

BURIED: Inglewood Park Cemetery, Los Angeles, California

■

HENRY DAVID THOREAU
1817—1862

Pencil maker and village crank, Thoreau was a professional bachelor who published only two small books, some poetry, and several essays during his lifetime. *Walden Pond*, a book about the two years he spent living in a shanty outside Concord, Massachusetts, is now considered one of the seminal books of the last century, and the principles in his essay "Civil Disobedience" were adopted by Gandhi and Martin Luther King, Jr. He died from a chill he caught while kneeling in the snow, counting the rings of a tree.

BURIED: Sleepy Hollow Cemetery, Concord, Massachusetts

■

BIG MAMA THORNTON
1926—1984

Big Mama was one of the great blues singers who paved the way for the emergence of rock and roll. On the road since the age of fourteen, she settled down in Texas in 1951, where three years later she was the first to record "Hound Dog," a song later immortalized by Elvis Presley.

BURIED: Inglewood Park Cemetery, Los Angeles, California

JIM THORPE
1888—1953

Called the greatest athlete of the twentieth century (for no compelling reason), he was the first Native American to become an Olympic champion. The two gold medals he won at the Stockholm Games were taken away from him by the Olympic committee after it was discovered that he had once played professional minor-league baseball. He tried his hand at acting in Hollywood for a few years but got just a few small roles playing Indians. When he died, his wife made a deal with the citizens of Mauch Chunk, Pennsylvania; she would bury him there only if they changed the name of the town to honor the athlete. They agreed.

BURIED: Thorpe Mausoleum, Jim Thorpe, Pennsylvania

ALICE B. TOKLAS
1877—1967

Longtime companion of Gertrude Stein, she wrote the famous cookbook that included a recipe for hashish brownies. One of the first organic gardeners, she cooked and served dinner for all the great writers and painters in their "charmed circle." She and Gertrude amassed a small fortune in art, buying modern masterpieces before anyone else. When Gertrude died, she left the paintings to Alice with the hope that she would be able to sell them, one by one, and live off the income. The Stein family thought otherwise and took Alice to court, successfully reversing the will, taking all the paintings and leaving Alice penniless. It is now believed by many that Alice was actually the coauthor of *The Autobiography of Alice B. Toklas*, Gertrude's highly successful account of their life together.

BURIED: Père Lachaise Cemetery, Paris, France

■

COUNT LEO TOLSTOY
1828—1910

Born into Russian nobility, orphaned at the age of nine, and raised by his aunts, Tolstoy fathered thirteen children while writing masterpieces like *War and Peace* and *Anna Karenina*. In 1876 he had a religious conversion, denounced his earlier work, renounced his wealth, and devoted the rest of his life to educating the serfs. He died in a train station, estranged from his family and adored by the common Russian people.

BURIED: Yasnaya Polyana, Tula, Russia

■

SPENCER TRACY
1900—1967

Known in Hollywood as the actor's actor, he began his film career playing gangsters, then priests, then finally the nice guys. Unwilling to divorce his Roman Catholic wife, he teamed up with the love of his life, Katharine Hepburn, and together they made many classic films, including *Adam's Rib, Keeper of the Flame,* and his final film, *Guess Who's Coming to Dinner?* Famous for describing his career as simply "a job," his talent is evident in a wide variety of films ranging from *Dr. Jekyll and Mr. Hyde* to *Judgment at Nuremberg*; he won the Oscar twice.

BURIED: Forest Lawn, Glendale, California

■

TRAVELLER

One of the heroes of the Civil War, General Lee's horse was his best friend and constant companion.

BURIED: Lee Chapel Museum, Washington & Lee University, Lexington, Virginia

■

TRIGGER

He was so loved by his owners, Roy Rogers and Dale Evans, that when this famous horse died, they (bless their little Hollywood hearts) had him stuffed, mounted, and put on display.

STUFFED: Roy Rogers, Dale Evans Museum, Victoryville, California

■

ANTHONY TROLLOPE
1815—1882

Writing forty-seven novels, including the Palliser and Barsetshire series, several books on travel, and collections of short stories, Anthony Trollope established the novel-sequence in English fiction. He wrote each morning before going to work at the post office, where he was credited with inventing the mailbox.

BURIED: Kensal Green Cemetery, London, England

FRANÇOIS TRUFFAUT
1932—1984

The seminal French film director gave us the classics *Jules & Jim* and *The 400 Blows* as well as an inspired acting performance in Spielberg's *Close Encounters of the Third Kind*.

BURIED: Montmartre Cemetery, Paris, France

DALTON TRUMBO
1906—1976

The most famous of the "Hollywood Ten," he was blacklisted and imprisoned for his political leanings during the Hollywood witch-hunts of the McCarthy period. Trumbo exiled himself to Mexico, where he continued to write scripts for the movies under various pseudonyms, including a screenplay for which he won an Academy Award. His book *Johnny Got His Gun*, a scathing antiwar novel that won the National Book Award in 1939, became a best-seller and a film during the Vietnam War.

BODY DONATED TO SCIENCE

■

HARRIET TUBMAN
1820—1913

Born a slave herself, this heroine of the abolitionist movement was called the Moses of her people. As the most successful "conductor" on the underground railroad, she led over three hundred slaves to freedom while serving the Union forces as a laundress, nurse, and spy.

BURIED: Fort Hill Cemetery, Cambridge, Massachusetts

■

FORREST TUCKER
1919—1986

Endowed with more than rugged good looks, he allegedly had the largest penis in Hollywood (a reputation that is apparently confirmed in the riding scene in the movie *Auntie Mame*). Tucker also starred briefly on television in *F Troop*.

BURIED: Forest Lawn Hollywood Hills, Los Angeles, California

■

SOPHIE TUCKER
1884—1966

"The Last of the Red Hot Mammas" was one of the biggest stars in vaudeville, and her ribald jokes were resurrected by none other than the Divine Miss M, Bette Midler, during her early career. Sophie appeared regularly on the "Ed Sullivan Show" and made a few forgettable films like *Follow the Boys* and *Broadway Melody of 1937*.

BURIED: Emanuel Cemetery, Wethersfield, Connecticut

■

MARK TWAIN
1835—1910

Printer, journalist, river pilot, and novelist, Samuel Clemens was an American original. His works, especially *Huckleberry Finn* and *Tom Sawyer*, have become classics, and his life story has become an American myth. He was, however, an extremely unhappy and bitter person whose writing creates an unflattering portrait of his fellow man. A financial failure despite his many successes, he had misanthropic and racist opinions that are repulsive to many of today's readers.

BURIED: Woodlawn Cemetery, Elmira, New York

TYPHOID MARY
1871—1903

Mary Malone knew only one thing: how to cook. Unfortunately, she was a carrier of typhoid fever, spreading the disease wherever she went. Not suffering from the disease herself, she continued to cook, jumping from job to job, leaving only after her employers began to get sick and die. She was caught by the authorities, incarcerated, and then released, promising she would never cook again. But she broke that promise, and more people died. Hunted down by the police and finally locked up for good, she died of a stroke after many years of incarceration.

BURIED: St. Raymond's Cemetery, Bronx, New York

MAURICE UTRILLO
1883–1955

One of the worst painters in history, this madman made a small fortune for his wife by selling his pastel-colored paintings of rain-drenched Paris, which he copied from postcards. Legally insane, he was often caught chasing pregnant women through the streets of Montmartre.

BURIED: St. Vincent Cemetery, Paris, France

■

RITCHIE VALENS
1941–1959

At the age of nine, Ritchie took up the guitar, then started his own band called the Silhouettes while still in high school. He was discovered playing at a school dance, signed to his first contract, and cut his first single, "Come On, Let's Go." His big success came next with "Donna" and "La Bamba." On his first national tour he flipped a coin with another performer to decide who would fly to the next stop. Ritchie won. The plane crashed, killing him along with Buddy Holly and The Big Bopper. Dead at the age of seventeen and with very little music recorded, he left a legacy that influenced a generation of other Chicano performers. Thirty years after his death, a movie based on his life was both a critical and financial success.

BURIED: Mission Hills Cemetery, San Fernando, California

■

RUDOLPH VALENTINO
1895—1926

Hollywood hack writers could not have written a better script than the one Valentino lived. A poor Italian immigrant, he arrived in Hollywood penniless, quickly became the biggest star of the silent screen, and died at the age of thirty-one from complications after surgery for a perforated ulcer. Twenty thousand fans rioted outside the New York City funeral home where he lay in state. When order was restored, over a hundred people were injured and the crowds continued to grow. Over ninety thousand people filed past his casket before his body was taken by train to Chicago, where it was viewed by thousands more. His death spawned a series of suicides among his fans, and for many years on the anniversary of his death the mysterious "woman in black" visited his grave to leave flowers.

BURIED: Hollywood Memorial Park Cemetery, Los Angeles, California

VINCENT VAN GOGH
1853—1889

What would Vincent say if he knew that one hundred years after his death one of his paintings sold for more than fifty million dollars? Penniless his entire life, he sold only one canvas during the short ten years he

painted, and that to his beloved brother, Theo. Van Gogh is thought to have been a manic depressive who, during his manic periods, would paint a picture a day as well as produce countless drawings and voluminous letters. He cut off his ear not after being rejected by a prostitute (as is commonly believed), but after an argument with Paul Gauguin, with whom he lived for a time. He painted up until and including the day he attempted suicide. He lived for several days after shooting himself but eventually succumbed to complications. His brother died a year later and is buried next to him.

BURIED: Churchyard Cemetery, Auvers, France

■

VIVIAN VANCE
1913—1979

Vivian Vance has achieved black-and-white immortality as Lucille Ball's sidekick and landlady, Ethel Mertz. Even though she never had to work again because of her royalties, she continued performing on the stage in summer theaters wherever and whenever they asked. She and her onscreen husband, William Frawley, were bitter enemies and never spoke to one another off the set.

CREMATED: Ashes scattered by friends

■

PAUL-MARIE VERLAINE
1844—1896

||||||||||||||||||||||||||||||||||||||||||||||||||||||||||||||||||||||||||||||||||||||||||||||||||||||||||

One of the great French poets, he left his wife and son for another young poet, Arthur Rimbaud. Their affair was a scandal and a disaster, ending with Verlaine's imprisonment for shooting Rimbaud in the wrist. Oddly enough, Verlaine did some of his best writing when confined and unable to obtain absinthe. He caught gonorrhea from Rimbaud and spent the last ten years of his life on public assistance in Paris hospitals, writing and holding court over a circle of visiting admirers.

BURIED: Batignolles Cemetery, Paris, France

■

VOLTAIRE
1694—1778

||||||||||||||||||||||||||||||||||||||||||||||||||||||||||||||||||||||||||||||||||||||||||||||||||||||||||

He was the father of the Enlightenment and spent his time either in favor with royalty at the Court or out of favor locked up in the Bastille. After he died, his writings fostered the French Revolution.

BURIED: The Pantheon, Paris, France

■

BILL W.
1895—1971

📖

He was the founder of Alcoholics Anonymous and the man described by Aldous Huxley as the "greatest social architect of our times."

BURIED: South Village Cemetery, East Dorset, Vermont

■

RICHARD WAGNER
1813—1883

Hitler's favorite composer was a genius whose life was awash in controversy. Banned from Bavaria for his anti-Semitism by the man who loved him (King Ludwig, the mad homosexual who built elaborate castles and showered his beloved with gold), Wagner settled in Switzerland for a time. Prodigiously talented, most of his operas are considered masterpieces, including *Tristan and Isolde, Parsifal, Tannhäuser,* and perhaps his greatest achievement of all, *The Ring Cycle* (*Das Rheingold, Die Walküre, Siegfried,* and *Götter-dämmerung*).

BURIED: Wahnfried Garden, Bayreuth, Germany

■

DINAH WASHINGTON
1924—1963

Born Ruth Jones in Tuscaloosa, Alabama, she moved to Chicago and began singing in the local Baptist church. She switched to secular music in 1942, joining the Lionel Hampton Band, where she quickly became a star. Her life was tumultuous, with seven marriages, a flaring temper, tacky wigs, and problems with drugs, alcohol, and the law. She died at the age of thirty-nine, leaving behind a legacy that continues to influence singers today.

BURIED: Burr Oak Cemetery, Alsip, Illinois

ANDY WARHOL
1927—1987

Nicknamed Drella, an apt combination of Dracula and Cinderella, he literally created an art based on worthlessness, allegedly not painting his own paintings, printing his own prints, or even signing them himself. His studio was called The Factory, and it churned out what can be viewed as souvenirs from the sixties and seventies, cleverly marketed as fine art. These products were snatched up by wealthy socialites who sold them back and forth to each other, inflating their value to ridiculous proportions. His other influence on culture, albeit unintentional, was in film. He turned the camera on and recorded the exhibitionism of his "friends," paying them twenty-five dollars a day while the films grossed millions. He carried a cassette recorder which he referred to as his wife, Sony, and taped his encounters with celebrities. These recordings became the basis for the highly successful magazine *Interview*. Carrying his money in small paper bags and ripping off the corners in order to keep track of expenses, he spent his days shopping. He survived a bizarre assassination attempt by Valerie Solanis only to die twenty years later under mysterious circumstances after minor surgery. The market value of his prints and paintings doubled the next day. Although he had several "boyfriends," he was apparently asexual as well as atalented.

BURIED: St. John the Baptist Cemetery, Bethel Park, Pennsylvania

■

ALAN WATTS
1915—1973

America's most articulate spokesperson for Zen Buddhism and Eastern spirituality, he was an eloquent, gentle man who chain-smoked and was frequently inebriated. He fathered seven children (on their eighteenth birthdays he gave them LSD and joined them on their first trips), had three wives, and still found time to write more than twenty books, including *The Way of Zen* and *The Book*.

CREMATED: Ashes interred behind the Zen Center, Green Gulch Farm, Stinson Beach, California

■

JOHN WAYNE
1907—1979

Hollywood's all-American cowboy, soldier, and rough-and-ready good guy, he always got the girl or whatever other prize was in the offing. Snubbed by the Oscars for years, he finally won for his eye-patched performance (again on horseback) in *True Grit*. In his private life he was a hawk on Vietnam, a friend and supporter of conservatives and Republican presidents and their causes, and a bane to the revolution of the 1960s. In a bizarre twist of fate, he was supposedly converted to Roman Catholicism on his deathbed, after spending his life denouncing organized religion.

BURIED: (with his boots on?) Pacific View Memorial Park, Newport Beach, California

■

CLIFTON WEBB
1889—1966

Webb was an acerbic actor whose brilliantly outrageous performance in *Laura* opened the closet door for previously veiled homosexual characters in Hollywood films. The opening scene in the film showed him sitting in an elaborate tub of steamy water with a bath tray arranged like a desk, commanding a fully dressed Dana Andrews to hand him his robe. An impeccable dresser, he was the epitome of the urbane gentleman who relied on his intellect and his cynicism to thrive and survive in a world filled with dunces.

BURIED: Hollywood Memorial Park, Los Angeles, California

■

JACK WEBB
1920—1982

As the unflappable Sergeant Joe Friday on television's "Dragnet," Webb became one of the most famous faces—and voices—in America during the heyday of television dramas.

BURIED: Forest Lawn Hollywood Hills, Los Angeles, California

■

NOAH WEBSTER
1758—1843

In 1828 Mr. Webster stunned the English-speaking world with his *American Dictionary of the English Language*. By recognizing American words and usage as valid, this work declared the linguistic independence of the United States from Britain. It is still a best-seller.

BURIED: Grove Street Cemetery, New Haven, Connecticut

■

KURT WEILL
1900—1950

As the musical collaborator of Bertolt Brecht, he invented a new art form called songspiel, which he used in *The Threepenny Opera* starring his wife, Lotte Lenya. It became the most successful musical in the history of German theater. Called Bolshevist madness at the time, the songs from the show became modern classics. Weill worked with Brecht also on *The Rise and Fall of the City of Mahagonny* and collaborated with Maxwell Anderson on *Knickerbocker Holiday*, a musical which includes his most famous composition, "September Song." His musical genius was evident once again in the psychological musical *Lady in the Dark* starring the incomparable Gertrude Lawrence.

BURIED: Mt. Repose Cemetery, Haverstraw, New York

JOHNNY WEISSMULLER
1904—1984

Winner of five gold medals at the Olympics in 1924 and 1928, Johnny Weissmuller racked up a total of fifty-two national championships and set sixty-seven world records before retiring from competition. Hollywood called, and he answered with a Tarzan yell. After he had made nineteen movies based on the character created by Edgar Rice Burroughs, the studios decided that he had become too old to play the apeman. He went on to make sixteen more films playing Jungle Jim.

BURIED: Valley of Light Cemetery, Acapulco, Mexico

■

MAE WEST
1893—1980

Starting in show business at the age of six, she became the highest-paid actress in Hollywood and one of the richest women in America. Playwright, Broadway star, sex symbol, and movie goddess, she was famous for injecting sexual innuendos into her scripts. She made her first movie when in her forties and was arrested and jailed for writing, producing, and starring in an "immoral" play called *Sex*. One of her most famous lines was "Come up and see me sometime," delivered to a young Cary Grant.

BURIED: Cypress Hills Cemetery, Brooklyn, New York

■

NATHANAEL WEST
1903—1940

Nicknamed Pep (because he had none), Nathanael West was lured to Hollywood after the critical success (but financial failure) of his first novel, *Miss Lonelyhearts*. He struggled for many years writing B movies while collecting material for his novel *Day of the Locust*. This book was a huge commercial flop but like *Lonelyhearts* became a classic after his death in an auto accident. Much to the surprise of his friends, he married Eileen McKenney (of *My Sister Eileen*), who was also killed in the accident. They are buried together, her ashes scattered in his coffin.

BURIED: Mt. Zion Cemetery, Maspeth, Long Island, New York

■

EDITH WHARTON
1862—1937

Her first book was a guide to interior decorating, which isn't surprising considering the environment in which she was raised, for Edith Wharton was born and reared in the upper-class circles of New York and Newport. What was there for her but a marriage and a home to decorate? Fortunately for American letters, she found marriage a severe disappointment and suffered several nervous breakdowns, divorced her husband, and moved to Paris, where she promptly fell in love with Henry James. The two traveled together as she continued to write using her own American experience in novels like *House of Mirth* and *Ethan Frome*, both of which were enormous best-sellers. She won the Pulitzer Prize in 1921 for *The Age of Innocence*.

BURIED: Protestant Cemetery, Versailles, France

∎

JAMES ABBOTT McNEILL WHISTLER
1834—1903

This American painter left the United States and lived his life in London and Paris (with his mother), where his work influenced not only other painters but writers as well. He is considered to be the inspiration for Proust's Elstir, and Oscar Wilde modeled the painter in *The Picture of Dorian Gray* after him. By all accounts Whistler was a paranoid, mean-spirited man, who betrayed his friends while accusing them of stealing his ideas. He was a prolific writer of scathing letters to the press about his contemporaries; these were published as a book called *The Gentle Art of Making Enemies*.

BURIED: St. Nicholas's Churchyard, Chiswick Mall, Chiswick, London, England

∎

WALT WHITMAN
1819—1892

One of the greatest of American poets, he published most of his work himself, achieving recognition only after Europeans began to recognize his talent and acknowledge his influence. He was born on Long Island and grew up in Brooklyn. His masterpiece, *Leaves of Grass*, appeared first as a book of 12 poems, then in its second edition with 21 poems. Its third edition contained 122 poems, including the group called Calamus, in which he celebrates his homosexuality—a remarkable thing to do in 1860. He spent the rest of his life revising and rewriting the work through six more editions. During the Civil War he worked as a hospital volunteer visiting the wounded. A stroke in 1873 left him paralyzed; he spent his final years living quietly and writing in Camden, New Jersey.

BURIED: Harleigh Cemetery, Camden, New Jersey

OSCAR WILDE
1854—1900

"I never travel without my diary," said Oscar Wilde; "one should always have something sensational to read." One of the great intellects of the nineteenth century, he was a brilliant classical scholar, winning honors for his keen intelligence as well as scorn for collecting blue pottery and peacock feathers during his student days at Oxford. He married and fathered two children before discovering his homosexuality, wrote art criticism, essays, poetry, novels, and plays. When he toured the United States (including the pioneer West), he was always greeted by cheering crowds but was disgraced in 1895 when sent to prison for committing sodomy with Lord Alfred Douglas. He was declared bankrupt while in jail, never recovered, and died several years later in Paris.

BURIED: Père Lachaise Cemetery, Paris, France

■

THORNTON WILDER
1897—1975

Successful as both a novelist with *The Bridge of San Luis Rey* and playwright with *Our Town*, he will probably be remembered most for being the original creator of the play that eventually became the musical *Hello, Dolly!* He worked as a screenwriter in Hollywood for a short time, but his alleged homosexuality upset the great studio heads, and he was forced out.

BURIED: Mt. Carmel Cemetery, Lyndhurst, New Jersey

■

HANK WILLIAMS
1923—1953

The king of country and western music, Williams recorded the classics "Your Cheatin' Heart," "Hey Good Lookin'," and "Cold Cold Heart" before dying of a heart attack.

BURIED: Oakwood Annex, Montgomery, Alabama

TENNESSEE WILLIAMS
1911—1983

One of the finest American playwrights, he spent his final decade trying to recapture the success of his early career. The man who wrote *Night of the Iguana*, *Sweet Bird of Youth*, *Suddenly Last Summer*, and *A Streetcar Named Desire* brought a raw yet sensitive realism to the stage and later to films. His work was filled with rape, cannibalism, drug addiction, and homosexuality. He survived countless failures, became an alcoholic, converted to Roman Catholicism, flaunted his sexuality, and finally choked to death on a bottle cap, alone in his apartment.

BURIED: Calvary Cemetery, St. Louis, Missouri

WALTER WINCHELL
1897—1972

Few people know that Walter Winchell began his career in vaudeville as part of a singing act that included George Jessel. He later became the most famous gossip columnist with "On Broadway" at the *New York Daily Mirror*. Early in his career he was a staunch supporter of Roosevelt and the New Deal, but later he did an about-face, became a far-right conservative, and supported Senator Joseph McCarthy's anticommunist witch-hunt. For a time he charmed the country with his distinctive voice on the radio, but he later used his powerful position in the media to spread fear by punishing those with whom he disagreed. Near the end of his life he narrated the hugely successful television show "The Untouchables."

BURIED: Greenwood Cemetery, Phoenix, Arizona

■

ANNA MAY WONG
1907—1961

Every studio needed a few ethnic personalities to play minor roles, and Wong was one of the best—so good that she developed a cult following that continues to this day because of her appearances in films like *The Thief of Bagdad*, *Shanghai Express*, and *Portrait in Black*, which was filmed a year before her death.

BURIED: Rosedale Cemetery, Los Angeles, California

■

THOMAS WOLFE
1900—1938

The author of *You Can't Go Home Again*, Thomas Wolfe was always going home in his writings; he wrote endlessly about his own short, alcoholic life and was so prolific that his manuscripts usually ran to a million words, all stuffed into several suitcases. It is doubtful that his work would have been enormously successful—bringing young Wolfe the money to drink himself to death—if it had not been for the herculean efforts of his editor, Maxwell Perkins, who turned the rambling pages into book form.

BURIED: Riverside Cemetery, Asheville, North Carolina

ALEXANDER WOOLLCOTT
1887—1943

Nicknamed "Louisa May Woollcott" by his friends, he was one of the founding editors of *The New Yorker* and was immortalized as the character Sheridan Whiteside in the Kaufman and Hart play *The Man Who Came to Dinner*. For years he held court at the the Algonquin Round Table, a group of New York intellectuals who lunched together daily in the hotel bar.

BURIED: Hamilton College, Clinton, New York

NATALIE WOOD
1938—1981

As a child in *Miracle on 34th Street* and then a teenager in *Rebel Without a Cause*, Natalie Wood was an international star until her sudden tragic death. In what was considered a freak accident, especially considering her lifelong fear of water, she somehow managed to fall off a yacht and drown while her husband, Robert Wagner, was on board sound asleep.

BURIED: Westwood Memorial Park, Los Angeles, California

■

VIRGINIA WOOLF
1882—1941

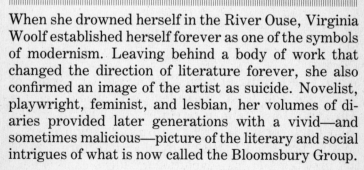

When she drowned herself in the River Ouse, Virginia Woolf established herself forever as one of the symbols of modernism. Leaving behind a body of work that changed the direction of literature forever, she also confirmed an image of the artist as suicide. Novelist, playwright, feminist, and lesbian, her volumes of diaries provided later generations with a vivid—and sometimes malicious—picture of the literary and social intrigues of what is now called the Bloomsbury Group.

CREMATED: Ashes buried by her husband, Leonard, under the great elm in the garden of Monkhouse, Rodmell, Sussex, England

■

THE WRIGHT BROTHERS
ORVILLE
1871—1948

WILBUR
1867—1912

The Wright brothers owned a successful chain of small bicycle shops but were consumed by the idea of flying. On December 17, 1903, they were the first to fly successfully a heavier-than-air machine, at Kitty Hawk, North Carolina. (Others had been aloft before in balloons.)

BURIED: Woodland Cemetery, Dayton, Ohio

■

FRANK LLOYD WRIGHT
1867—1959

When a new wing of a building at the University of Wisconsin collapsed, a student who would become America's most famous architect decided to switch from engineering to architecture, and applied engineering principles to the study of architecture. One of the first tests of his revolutionary ideas came when, shortly after he built the first earthquake-proof building in Tokyo, the city was leveled; only his Imperial Hotel was still standing. His most unusual building is the Guggenheim Museum in New York City. The original plans called for gilding the round exterior, and, since he hated painting, he designed the interior in such a way that it is almost impossible to hang pictures. His proposal for a one-mile-high skyscraper reflected not his genius but his monumental ego.

BURIED: Jones Family Cemetery, Spring Green, Wisconsin

■

MALCOLM X (EL-HAJJ MALIK EL-SHABAZZ)
1925—1965

The assassination of Malcolm X on February 21, 1965, in Harlem's Audubon Ballroom silenced one of the most intelligent and honest voices in America. Born into poverty and schooled in crime, Malcolm X discovered the teachings of Elijah Muhammad while in prison. Once released, he became the articulate spokesperson and recruiter for the organization, swelling the membership from about four hundred to forty thousand. It was during a trip to Mecca in 1964 that Malcolm began his intellectual journey away from the Nation of Islam. Unfortunately, it was a journey that would lead to his murder. Twenty thousand people of all races filed past his coffin as he lay in state in Harlem. His life and words live on primarily in the book *The Autobiography of Malcolm X*, written by the author of *Roots*, Alex Haley.

BURIED: Ferncliff Cemetery, Hartsdale, New York

■

BRIGHAM YOUNG
1801—1877

This young carpenter was converted by Joseph Smith's brother and soon thereafter appointed one of the twelve Apostles of the Mormon Church. He led his followers to Utah, where he was appointed governor by President Fillmore. When he died, it was discovered that he had amassed a personal fortune of over two-and-one-half million dollars. His survivors included seventeen wives and fifty-six children.

BURIED: Brigham Young Cemetery, Salt Lake City, Utah

■

DARRYL F. ZANUCK
1902—1979

From hack film writer of the Rin Tin Tin movies to founder of Twentieth Century-Fox, this winner of the first Irving Thalberg Award produced some of the finest American films including *The Grapes of Wrath*, *The Adventures of Sherlock Holmes*, *Young Mr. Lincoln*, and *All About Eve*. He also produced some of the worst. During the filming of one of these clinkers, *The Roots of Heaven*, in Africa, he arranged with the local mother superior of a Catholic hospital to supply Errol Flynn with all the heroin he needed in exchange for a new wing on the nun's hospital. He once threatened

Bette Davis, whom he had made a star, with the now famous words, "You'll never work in this town again." He is also credited with discovering Marilyn Monroe.

BURIED: Westwood Memorial Park, Los Angeles, California

■

FLORENZ ZIEGFELD
1869—1932

Would the world have ever known Fanny Brice, Will Rogers, Eddie Cantor, Mae West, Marilyn Miller, or W. C. Fields if Flo Ziegfeld had not given them center stage on Broadway in his extravagant annual musical revues? Whatever the answer, there can be no denying that it was on the stage of the New Amsterdam Theater in the Ziegfeld Follies that they and many other show business greats got their starts. A generous and trusting man, Flo Ziegfeld had no written contracts with his stars; one by one they deserted him for lucrative film careers in the golden hills of California. He was ruined by the stock market crash of the twenties, and except for a brief partnership with Sam Goldwyn in Hollywood, his career as the greatest Broadway producer never recovered.

BURIED: Kensico Cemetery, Valhalla, New York

■

APPENDIX
A GEOGRAPHICAL LISTING
OF WHO'S WHERE

ALABAMA
Hank Williams

ARKANSAS
Martha Mitchell

ARIZONA
Walter Winchell

CALIFORNIA
Gracie Allen
Mary Astor
Jim Backus
Lucille Ball
Lionel Barrymore
Wallace Beery
Bea Benaderet
Jack Benny
Edgar Bergen
Clara Blandick
Humphrey Bogart
Ray Bolger
Clara Bow
Charles Boyer
Fanny Brice
Lenny Bruce
Nigel Bruce
Sebastian Cabot
Godfrey Cambridge
Eddie Cantor
Truman Capote
Karen Carpenter
John Cassavetes
Jeff Chandler
Raymond Chandler
Lon Chaney, Sr.
Lee J. Cobb
Nat "King" Cole

Jackie Coogan
Lou Costello
Bing Crosby
Dorothy Dandridge
Bette Davis
Sammy Davis, Jr.
Cecil B. DeMille
Walt Disney
Margaret Dumont
Dominique Dunne
Will and Ariel Durant
Jimmy Durante
Nelson Eddy
Marty Feldman
W. C. Fields
Peter Finch
Larry Fine
Errol Flynn
John Ford
William Frawley
Clark Gable
Janet Gaynor
Gorgeous George
Andy Gibb
Hermione Gingold
Samuel Goldwyn
Betty Grable
Sydney Greenstreet
Joan Hackett
Jack Haley
Oliver Hardy
Jean Harlow
Gabby Hayes
Rita Hayworth
William Randolph Hearst
Woody Herman
Conrad Hilton
Jerome and Shemp Howard
John Huston
George Jessel
Al Jolson
Spike Jones
Buster Keaton

CALIF. (cont.)

Percy Kilbride
Ernie Kovacs
Alan Ladd
Mario Lanza
Charles Laughton
Stan Laurel
Oscar Levant
Liberace
Diane Linkletter
Carole Lombard
Jack London
Peter Lorre
Bela Lugosi
Chico Marx
Groucho Marx
Louis B. Mayer
Hattie McDaniel
Jeanette MacDonald
Fibber McGee and Molly
Adolph Menjou
Tom Mix
Marilyn Monroe
Alla Nazimova
Ozzie Nelson
Ramon Novarro
Clifford Odets
Roy Orbison
Louella Parsons
Petey
Zasu Pitts
Eleanor Powell
Tyrone Power
Freddie Prinze
George Raft
Sally Rand
Donna Reed
George Reeves
Rin Tin Tin
Rosalind Russell
Sabu
Edie Sedgwick
David O. Selznick
Norma Shearer
Bugsy Siegel
Phil Silvers
John Steinbeck (monument)
Max Steiner
Dorothy Stratten
Levi Strauss

Sharon Tate
Irving Thalberg
William "Buckwheat"
  Thomas
Big Mama Thornton
Spencer Tracy
Trigger
Forrest Tucker
Ritchie Valens
Rudolph Valentino
Alan Watts
John Wayne
Clifton Webb
Jack Webb
Anna May Wong
Natalie Wood
Darryl F. Zanuck

CONNECTICUT

P. T. Barnum
Raymond Massey
Frederick Law Olmsted
Sophie Tucker
Noah Webster

FLORIDA

Rocky Marciano

GEORGIA

Billy Carter
Lillian Carter
Susan Hayward
Martin Luther King, Jr.
Margaret Mitchell
Ma Rainey

HAWAII

Charles Lindbergh

IDAHO

Ernest Hemingway

ILLINOIS

Al Capone
Richard J. Daley

Emma Goldman
Abraham Lincoln
Mary Todd Lincoln
Morris the Cat
Elijah Muhammad
Jesse Owens
Jack Ruby
Robert Stroud
Dinah Washington

INDIANA

Johnny Appleseed
Hoagy Carmichael
James Dean
John Dillinger
Emmett Kelly
Alfred Kinsey
Cole Porter

KANSAS

Comanche

KENTUCKY

Edgar Cayce
D. W. Griffith
Man O' War
Thomas Merton

LOUISIANA

Mahalia Jackson

MARYLAND

Tallulah Bankhead
John Wilkes Booth
F. Scott Fitzgerald
Zelda Fitzgerald
Dorothy Parker
Edgar Allan Poe

MASSACHUSETTS

Louisa May Alcott
Horatio Alger
John Belushi
Lizzie Borden

John Cheever
e e cummings
Albert De Salvo
Emily Dickinson
Mary Baker Eddy
Fannie Farmer
Buckminster Fuller
Lillian Hellman
Hans Hoffman
Winslow Homer
Henry James
Jack Kerouac
Gertrude Lawrence
Henry Wadsworth
  Longfellow
Cotton Mather
Warner Oland
Eugene O'Neill
Norman Rockwell
Harriet Beecher Stowe
Henry David Thoreau
Harriet Tubman

MISSISSIPPI

William Faulkner
Robert Johnson

MISSOURI

Jesse James
Carry Nation
Satchel Paige
Charlie Parker
Tennessee Williams

MONTANA

Smokey the Bear

NEW HAMPSHIRE

Grace Metalious
Claude Rains

NEW JERSEY

Thomas Alva Edison
John O'Hara

NEW JERSEY (cont.)

Walt Whitman
Thornton Wilder

NEW MEXICO

Billy the Kid
D. H. Lawrence

NEW YORK

Susan B. Anthony
Fatty Arbuckle
Hannah Arendt
Louis Armstrong
John James Audubon
James Baldwin
George Balanchine
Leonard Bernstein
John Brown
Mother Cabrini
James Cagney
William Casey
Checkers
Montgomery Clift
John Coltrane
Terence Cardinal Cooke
Joan Crawford
Jackie Curtis
George Custer
Candy Darling
Frederick Douglass
Ethyl Eichelberger
Duke Ellington
Fala
Joey Gallo
John Garfield
Judy Garland
Lou Gehrig
George Gershwin
Peggy Guggenheim
Lorraine Hansberry
Abbie Hoffman
Billie Holiday
Judy Holliday
Edward Hopper
Harry Houdini
Langston Hughes
Washington Irving
Dorothy Kilgallen

Fiorello La Guardia
Bert Lahr
Lotte Lenya
Charles Ludlam
"Moms" Mabley
Herman Melville
Sal Mineo
Thelonious Monk
Grandma Moses
Frank O'Hara
Jackson Pollock
Sergei Rachmaninoff
Ayn Rand
Basil Rathbone
Paul Robeson
Bill "Bojangles" Robinson
Edward G. Robinson
Jackie Robinson
Nelson Rockefeller
Eleanor Roosevelt
Theodore Roosevelt
Ethel and Julius Rosenberg
Mark Rothko
Babe Ruth
Diana Sands
Margaret Higgins Sanger
Rod Serling
Bishop Fulton J. Sheen
Kate Smith
Francis Cardinal Spellman
Ed Sullivan
Herbert Tarnower
Mark Twain
Typhoid Mary
Kurt Weill
Mae West
Nathanael West
Alexander Woollcott
Malcolm X
Florenz Ziegfeld

NORTH CAROLINA

Ava Gardner
Thomas Wolfe

OHIO

Annie Oakley
Orville and Wilbur Wright

OKLAHOMA

Geronimo

PENNSYLVANIA

Pearl Bailey
Ethel Barrymore
John Barrymore
Pearl S. Buck
Jim Croce
Father Divine
Thomas Eakins
Zane Grey
Franz Kline
Mary Jo Kopechne
Jayne Mansfield
Margaret Mead
Horace Pippin
Betsy Ross
Bessie Smith
Jim Thorpe
Andy Warhol

RHODE ISLAND

Anaïs Nin

SOUTH DAKOTA

Sitting Bull

TENNESSEE

Elvis Presley

TEXAS

Clyde Barrow
Buddy Holly
Lee Harvey Oswald
Bonnie Parker
Karen Silkwood

UTAH

Brigham Young

VERMONT

Robert Frost
Bill W.

VIRGINIA

Patsy Cline
Medgar Evers
Virgil "Gus" Grissom
Dashiell Hammett
John F. Kennedy
Robert E. Lee
Joe Louis
Audie Murphy
Traveller

WASHINGTON

Jimi Hendrix
Bruce Lee

WASHINGTON, D.C.

J. Edgar Hoover
Helen Keller
Charlie McCarthy

WISCONSIN

George Gipp
Alfred Lunt and Lynn
    Fontanne
Joseph McCarthy
Frank Lloyd Wright

AUSTRIA

W. H. Auden
Ludwig van Beethoven

BRAZIL

Carmen Miranda

CANADA

Alexander Graham Bell

CZECHOSLOVAKIA

Franz Kafka

ENGLAND

Jane Austen
Robert Browning

ENGLAND (cont.)

Lord Byron
Agatha Christie
Winston Churchill
Charles Darwin
Charles Dickens
Lord Alfred Douglas
George Eliot
T. S. Eliot
Sigmund Freud
Radclyffe Hall
Aldous Huxley
Brian Jones
Karl Marx
Laurence Olivier
Sylvia Plath
Pocahontas
George Bernard Shaw
Anthony Trollope
James Abbott McNeill
  Whistler
Virginia Woolf

FRANCE

Marie Antoinette
Honoré de Balzac
Charles Baudelaire
Aubrey Beardsley
Simone de Beauvoir
Samuel Beckett
Sarah Bernhardt
Napoleon Bonaparte
Albert Camus
Mary Cassatt
Maurice Chevalier
Frédéric Chopin
Jean Cocteau
Colette
Claude Debussy
Edgar Degas
Isadora Duncan
Gustave Flaubert
Dr. Joseph Ignace Guillotine
Victor Hugo
Henri Matisse
Jean Baptiste
Jim Morrison
Vaslav Nijinsky

Edith Piaf
Pablo Picasso
Marcel Proust
Maurice Ravel
Auguste Rodin
Jean-Paul Sartre
Jean Seberg
Eddie Slovik
Chaim Soutine
Gertrude Stein
Alice B. Toklas
François Truffaut
Maurice Utrillo
Vincent Van Gogh
Paul-Marie Verlaine
Voltaire
Edith Wharton
Oscar Wilde

GERMANY

Bertolt Brecht
The Brothers Grimm
Richard Wagner

GHANA

W.E.B. DuBois

GREECE

Aristotle Onassis

IRELAND

Brendan Behan

ITALY

Elizabeth Barrett Browning
Enrico Caruso
Sergei Diaghilev
Vladimir Horowitz
John Keats
Sinclair Lewis
Alberto Moravia
Pope Pius XII
Ezra Pound

Sacco & Vanzetti
Percy Bysshe Shelley
Igor Stravinsky

JAMAICA

Sir Noel Coward
Bob Marley

MEXICO

Frida Kahlo
Diego Rivera
Johnny Weissmuller

MONACO

Grace Kelly

THE NETHERLANDS

Rembrandt Van Rijn

NORWAY

Sonja Henie

RUSSIA

Anton Chekhov
Sergei Eisenstein
Nikolai Gogol
Nikita Khrushchev
Vladimir Lenin
John Reed
Joseph Stalin
Count Leo Tolstoy

SPAIN

Christopher Columbus
Salvador Dali

SWITZERLAND

Richard Burton
Coco Chanel
Charles Chaplin
Hermann Hesse

James Joyce
Vladimir Nabokov

TAHITI

Paul Gauguin

WALES

Dylan Thomas

DONATED TO SCIENCE

Spring Byington
Bobby Darin
Dalton Trumbo

ASHES SCATTERED

Bud Abbott (Pacific Ocean)
Ansel Adams (Yosemite)
Ingrid Bergman (Sweden)
Maria Callas (Aegean Sea)
Wally Cox (Massachusetts)
Albert Einstein (New Jersey)
"Mama" Cass Elliot (Pacific Ocean)
Malcolm Forbes (Fiji)
E. M. Forster (England)
Mahatma Gandhi (India)
Gary Gilmore (Utah)
Cary Grant (ashes remain with widow)
Woody Guthrie (Atlantic Ocean)
Bruno Richard Hauptmann (Germany)
Adolf Hitler (Germany)
Rock Hudson (Pacific Ocean)
Jim Jones (at sea)
Janis Joplin (Pacific Ocean)
Veronica Lake (Caribbean)
Elsa Lanchester (at sea)
Vivien Leigh (England)
John Lennon (England and New York)
Leonardo da Vinci (France)

ASHES SCATTERED (cont.)

Steve McQueen (California)
Harvey Milk (California)
Henry Miller (California)
Charles Mingus (India)
Adam Clayton Powell, Jr.
  (Bimini)

Barbara Stanwyck (Pacific
  Ocean)
John Steinbeck (Pacific
  Ocean)
Vivian Vance (ashes scat-
  tered by friends)